Praise for

INDIE SPIRITUALIST

from Awesome People of All Walks of Life

"Chris Grosso seamlessly blends the ideas of individuality and spirituality in a way that is selfless, easy to read, and inspiring. He can help you find a purpose and be proud of yourself."
—**Tony Hawk**, skateboarding icon

"Those of us who are muddling and meandering our way along a spiritual path often wind up befuddled, a bit lost, and in need of guidance from someone with the chops to light the path so that we can find our own way. Chris Grosso is just such a light-bearer. With his own quirky breed of indie spiritualism, Chris seeks the sublime and invites us to seek it for ourselves. His book, *Indie Spiritualist,* will be a great service to those looking outside traditional religious paths to find divinity within themselves and in the world."
—**Lissa Rankin**, MD, *New York Times* bestselling author of *Mind Over Medicine*

"Chris writes from the inside out about learning to love without holding back. This book is alive with truth-telling: It is a transmission that will turn you towards the light of your own awakening heart."
—**Tara Brach, PhD**, author of *Radical Acceptance* and *True Refuge*

"You awaken your true spirit by way of the broken heart: ragged, vulnerable, fierce, and, finally, compassionate. Christ trod this rough way and shows honestly how it can be done."
—**Jack Kornfield**, bestselling author of *A Path with Heart*

"*Indie Spiritualist* offers clear insight and fresh inspiration for this emerging generation of truth seekers. It's a great read and serves as a good friend to have along the path."
—**MC Yogi**, hip-hop artist, graffiti writer, and yoga teacher

"Chris Grosso, in a well written book, takes us into his mind and through a plethora of experiences. *Indie Spiritualist* guides readers to a greater awareness and love for themselves and others."
—**Ram Dass**, author of *Be Here Now*

"*Indie Spiritualist*, by my dear friend Chris Grosso, cuts right to the heart of what engaged Dharma Buddhism is all about, while sparing the bullshit. Chris's writing, while relevant for all readers, does something most contemporary spiritual teachers don't, and that is make spirituality accessible for our youth, especially the inner city homies who are thirsty for it but need the message straight up. Thank you Chris for this book, which is sure to change the lives of those who read it."
—**Jarvis Jay Masters**, author of *That Bird Has My Wings* and *Finding Freedom*

"This is ragged truth-telling at its best, and Chris speaks directly from nothing but his own experience. It is therefore as honest and authentic an account of spirituality as you will likely find anywhere. What else could you ask for? We have known for some time now that the spirituality of tomorrow will not be your father's spirituality—it will be different; it will be wilder; it will be more direct; it will be more real and authentic; it will speak, not of creeds or beliefs, but directly to the heart and mind in the most certain and unmistakable words imaginable. In other words, it will speak a lot like this book does. Pick it up; read it; find out for yourself; and you'll be very glad you did."
—**Ken Wilber**, author of *The Integral Vision*

"Chris Grosso is a caring and compassionate human being who can also be relied upon to do things right. I have worked with him and can verify that he comes from his heart while maintaining the ability to use his intellect and intuition to make the right choices and do the right things."

—**Bernie Siegel**, MD, bestselling author of
Love, Medicine, and Miracles

"Chris Grosso's message is simple: dogma-free spirituality that's available to everyone, at all times. Whether you're attending a meditation event, a rock concert, a yoga class, or even a rehab program, spirit is always accessible. I'm grateful for what I've learned from Chris, and I'm excited to see the impact that his wisdom and work will undoubtedly have on the world."

—**Marci Shimoff**, *New York Times* bestselling author of
Love for No Reason and *Happy for No Reason*

"Chris Grosso shares his life experiences and spiritual awakening with depth, clarity, humility, and understanding. Chris's words are equally tangible for "lost soul" teens that are completely dissatisfied with the world, longtime spiritual practitioners, and those just looking for something more. Chris has truly given us a useful gift."

—**Jessica Pimentel**, actress (*Orange Is the New Black*),
Tibetan Buddhist, and musician (Alekhine's Gun)

"Every generation finds a voice that speaks their language while also sharing the wisdom of the past. Chris Grosso is that voice for our generation, as he speaks the wisdom we need to hear while weaving in real life. *Indie Spiritualist* is practical, heartfelt, and the truest of truths."

—**Betsy Chasse**, author of *Tipping Sacred Cows* and cocreator of
What The Bleep Do We Know!? and *What The Bleep?! Now What!?*

"There's a new generation of spiritualist emerging, and Chris's work on his website, *The Indie Spiritualist*, has established him as a leading visionary among them. We believe there is no better voice than Chris's for this project, and know that this book will be of great support to all who seek wisdom."

—**Stephen and Ondrea Levine**, bestselling authors of *Embracing the Beloved, Who Dies?* and *The Grief Process*

"Chris Grosso and his book *Indie Spiritualist* ain't going nowhere. Feel the vibe or get left behind."

—**Treach**, Naughty by Nature

"[The Indie Spiritualist] website is an edgy field of delights. [Chris's] interview questions set me thinking in new directions. I have found his website . . . to be an interesting attempt to capture the Spirit of the times: timely, timeless, and otherwise."

—**Lama Surya Das**, bestselling author of *Awakening the Buddha Within*

"Chris Grosso walks us through his own experiences, devoid of grandiosity, and with a sense of knowing that each answer gained unravels further inquiries and opportunities for self-exploration. Thank you, Chris, for an entertaining and smart read."

—**Gavin Van Vlack**, founding member of legendary NYC hardcore bands Burn and Absolution

"Chris Grosso is a humble, wise, penetrating writer and spiritual pioneer. I tremendously enjoyed the range and depth of *Indie Spiritualist* and found myself drawn into unsuspected mysteries and depths. I believe his book will be immensely useful, accessible, and a source of joy to many seekers."

—**Andrew Harvey**, bestselling author of *The Hope*

"*Indie Spiritualist* holds great tidings. It's not the usual cautionary tale—*don't try this at home*—of addiction and recovery. Chris sets a high-bar, combining authenticity with concise, wise self-reflection, which inspires us to consider our own experience and find our own spiritual truth. There is great spaciousness in *Indie Spiritualist*. Here's your permission to be you."
—**Tommy Rosen**, yoga teacher, addiction/recovery expert, and author of *Recovery 2.0*

"Chris Grosso has written a rowdy and real guide to spiritual practice that avoids the fluff and 'fast food for the mind' rhetoric that one so often finds in the 'spirituality' section of bookstores these days. *Indie Spiritualist* is highly recommended for those who are serious about spirituality and not just looking for a happy pill to make it all better."
—**Brad Warner**, bestselling author of *Hardcore Zen* and *Sit Down and Shut Up*

"Chris Grosso shares a message from the heart with honesty and deep awareness. He has created a masterpiece of art, an expression of his love. *Indie Spiritualist* brings us a beautiful introduction to a new era of spirituality."
—**don Jose Ruiz**, *New York Times* bestselling coauthor of *The Fifth Agreement* with don Miguel Ruiz

INDIE
SPIRITUALIST

INDIE SPIRITUALIST

a no bullshit exploration of spirituality

CHRIS GROSSO

Foreword by Noah Levine, author of *Dharma Punx*

ATRIA PAPERBACK
New York London Toronto Sydney New Delhi

BEYOND WORDS
Hillsboro, Oregon

ATRIA PAPERBACK
A Division of Simon & Schuster, Inc.
1230 Avenue of the Americas
New York, NY 10020

BEYOND WORDS
20827 N.W. Cornell Road, Suite 500
Hillsboro, Oregon 97124-9808
503-531-8700 / 503-531-8773 fax
www.beyondword.com

Audio podcast interview with Noah Levine and video interview with Ram Dass courtesy of *Where Is My Guru* radio show.

"Transistor," from the EP *Where Moths Eat and Worms Destroy*, and "Invocation," from the EP *Invocation: Our Dying Days*, by Womb of the Desert Sun, courtesy of The Path Less Traveled Records, www.thepathlesstraveledrecords.com.

All other songs written and performed by Chris Grosso, including: "A Little Less Like Dying," "All About Us," "Cardboard Suitcase," "The Complete Fiction," "Drawing Static," "Hand of the Host," "The Last Night of the Earth," "Perils of the Living," "Places That Scare You," "Rising/Falling," and "Scream Phoenix."

Managing Editor: Lindsay S. Brown
Editors: Henry Covey, Emily Han
Copyeditor: Sheila Ashdown
Proofreader: Mark Antonides
Cover Design: Trent Debord
Interior Design: Devon Smith
Author Photo: Breeze Floyd
Composition: William H. Brunson Typography Services

First Atria Paperback/Beyond Words trade paperback edition March 2014

For more information about special discounts for bulk purchases, please contact Simon & Schuster Special Sales at 1-866-506-1949 or business@simonandschuster.com.

The Simon & Schuster Speakers Bureau can bring authors to your live event. For more information or to book an event, contact the Simon & Schuster Speakers Bureau at 1-866-248-3049 or visit our website at www.simonspeakers.com.

Manufactured in the United States of America

10 9 8 7 6 5 4 3 2 1

Library of Congress Cataloging-in-Publication Data

Grosso, Chris.
    Indie spiritualist : a no bullshit exploration of spirituality / Chris Grosso.
        pages   cm
    Includes bibliographical references.
    1. Spirituality.   2. Spiritual life.   I. Title.
    BL624.G766   2014
    204—dc23

                                    2013041880

ISBN 978-1-58270-462-3
ISBN 978-1-4767-4708-8 (ebook)

The corporate mission of Beyond Words Publishing, Inc.: *Inspire to Integrity*

For Mom, Dad, and Jay—
Thank you for your unconditional love
and support through even the
darkest nights of my soul.

And for Jenn and Morgan (Momotron)—
You guys are my heart, my Jedi, my inspiration.
I love you both so much.

CONTENTS

 Angels of Darkness (The Words, The Ways)

B Demons of Light (Meditations, Practices, and Multimedia Suggestions)

Meditations

Practices

Eclectic Multimedia Suggestions

FOREWORD

All beings have taken birth to experience healing and freedom from suffering. This is the universal and undeniable truth. We wander through the realms of existence, states of mind, cultural conditions, and generations, seeking a reliable refuge. Some find comfort in religion; some find comfort in material success. But neither religion nor material success offers a reliable shelter. The Buddha referred to both religion and materialism as "dead ends." He found a path that led between these two extremes, the "middle path," the path of awakening and healing, a personal path that has little to do with religiosity or materialism. The healing we took birth for is attained by those who reject the norms, reject the world's false promises of pleasure-based happiness. It is not by reliance on external conditions, but by becoming independently committed to truth, kindness, compassion, and wisdom, that we find what we have always been seeking.

The Buddha was an "indie spiritualist"; he walked away from

reject the world's false promises

the spiritual and religious circles of his time and found his own path. The Buddha urged his students to reject all blind faith and cultural traditions based on what was written, spoken, or believed by others. He encouraged personal and independent investigation of spiritual matters. He basically said: "Try it for yourself, and trust your own direct experience. If the path that you are on leads to suffering and confusion, abandon it. If the path that you are on leads to freedom and well-being, follow it to the end." Later teachers have summed this up as, "Don't become a Buddhist; become a Buddha."

My teacher Jack Kornfield has often spoken about finding a "path with heart." What we need most is not more religious dogma

compassion is a skill

and spiritual materialism, but to train our hearts and minds to meet the reality of our lives in a wise and compassionate way. Compassion is a skill that we develop over time and with our own efforts. Wisdom comes when we learn to look within, when we turn toward the pain and confusion in our hearts. Then the heart becomes the path, and the path becomes the training of the heart and mind to be kind. His Holiness the Dalai Lama has been quoted as saying, "Kindness is my religion." Kindness is like situational ethics; the kind thing to do in each moment depends on what is happening right now. Kindness is not always nice or gentle. Sometimes it is loud and aggressive, like when we need to turn up the music loud enough to disturb the reactive habitual conditioning of the mind. Sometimes the kind thing to do is be generous and give to someone in need. At other times the kindest thing we can do is say "No!" The meditative training of the mind will, eventually, allow us to access the kind and wise heart.

In this open, honest, and wise reflection on his path, Chris Grosso offers us his heart. His search for meaning and recovery led him to a "path with heart." His explorations, practices, and awakenings are hard won and directly experienced. Chris does not sit back and talk about stuff he has heard or read. This is not an intellectual exercise; this is a direct transmission of his personal path of spiritual transformation. The core teaching here is not "do what I do," it is "find out for yourself what works."

May this book inspire you to become independently wise and compassionate. May you do what needs to be done in your own life to end suffering and confusion. Together may we all create a positive change in this world.

Yours in the spiritual revolution,
Noah Levine
2013

PREFACE:
Scream Phoenix

If you're going to try, go all the way.
There is no other feeling like that.
You will be alone with the gods,
and the nights will flame with fire.
You will ride life straight to perfect laughter.
It's the only good fight there is.

Charles Bukowski

"**H**ope, it's the last to die," said an elderly man sitting across from me some years ago on a bus in Rome at 2:00 AM. He'd just read the word *hope* tattooed across my knuckles, and I have to say that, in my own personal life experience, man, was he right. Life is full of terror and beauteous rapture, and I've experienced both on numerous occasions. From a life filled with despair, jail, emergency rooms, detoxes, and rehabs, to one of hope.

"Sex, drugs, and rock 'n' roll" really was the clichéd mantra of my younger years. It began as an innocent yet angsty kinship with grunge, punk, and hardcore music, which I fell in love with from the very first time I put needle to record. A friend of a friend described the punk/hardcore scene as "a last-ditch effort for authenticity in a world increasingly devoid of it," and I'd have to agree. There were groups discussing all sorts of relevant topics in their lyrics, from politics to personal ethics, spirituality, and all the "isms" you can think of. This had a huge effect on me. Not only did it teach me to question authority, to not accept everything at face value—which popular society and mass media would obviously prefer we do—but it was the first time that I ever really felt as though I was a part of something bigger than myself.

I'll admit that I was young and naïve and didn't totally understand what I was rebelling against a lot of the time. It was still, however, an amazing lesson in freeing myself from what others thought—albeit often on a superficial level—but it helped me find my own voice and truth, and take stands where others wouldn't. This definitely didn't earn me any cool points. With my tattoos, piercings, and punk T-shirts, I stood out like a sore thumb in my small town. But I didn't give a shit about that, as punk/hardcore music taught me not to cave to peer pressure like many other students would.

This music and sense of community quickly sparked my interest in learning to play bass and guitar so that I too could be on stage like the bands that I admired. I didn't have lofty dreams of reaching Soundgarden's level or being on MTV, but I did think it'd be great to make it to the level of a band like Converge, who were signed to a reputable indie label and had the ability to tour both nationally and internationally. While some of my bands did release CDs and seven inches on smaller indie labels, and even had a coveted merch table filled with T-shirts, stickers, and so forth, I still never made it anywhere close to where I'd hopefully envisioned myself.

That didn't stop my emulation of what many see as the classic rock 'n' roll lifestyle, however. I started experimenting with drugs and alcohol later than most of the kids I went to school with, because I spent my freshman and sophomore years as "straight edge" (which means living drug, alcohol, and nicotine free, sometimes even abstaining from sex, though the latter was a little much for me). It was late in my junior year that I decided to "break edge," and, like a sledgehammer to concrete, I broke the shit out of it. I started with pot and alcohol, like most experimental kids do, but it wasn't long before I ventured into the very strange and exciting world of mushrooms and LSD.

From drug free, I quickly made my way through the stages of drug use, including experimentation, regular use, abuse, and, finally, full-on addiction. What started as an occasional beer and joint at practice or before a show quickly turned into tripping on acid and mushrooms, sniffing cocaine and Ritalin, and spending plenty of time getting fucked up on ketamine, PCP, OxyContin, and crack. Oh, and of course there was always enough liquor to get a small army drunk. And so it was in my late teens that I became a full-blown (albeit functioning) addict.

Blackouts, hangovers, broken instruments, and terrible, drunk live performances became the norm. At one point my indie rock band Three Ways Till Tuesday was banned from playing every club, large and small—with the exception of friends' basements or VFW halls—in our home state of Connecticut, due to our drug and alcohol fueled antics. We even blew a $10,000 indie record deal (which was a lot of money for us at the time) when we showed up wasted to a show that the label owner had set up as a sort of showcase for his friends and colleagues. I vaguely remember setting up my guitar amp that night, but that's it. The next morning I awoke with an odd bruise on my forehead, which I later found out was due to my repeatedly smashing myself in the head with my microphone during our set. I turned on my phone and received a frantic voicemail from the label owner, screaming, "What the fuck happened last night?! What is wrong with you guys?! The deal's off!" And the saddest thing about this story is that it's only the tip of the iceberg.

That sort of blackout drinking and drug-addicted behavior carried on for some years until, at the age of twenty-four, it all came to a head. Fear, anger, hurt, sadness, drugs, empty sex, food, cutting, and suicide attempts—all culminated in a perfect storm, a tempest that shattered my heart and left me nothing more than the shell of a man. In my broken state, I had **a tempest that shattered my heart** nothing left to lose. I was brought to my knees by my addiction and knew that if I was going to live, I needed to surrender and find a new way to live life. Every part of my physical self was ready to die and welcomed the thought of death. But inside, a small flame flickered. It was very faint and very deep, yet it was enough that, no matter how hard I tried to ignore it, I couldn't; it wouldn't let me. Hope.

I finally checked into a detox unit. While there I quickly realized it was the first time I'd been without a drug for more than a day or so in many years. I'd known for a while that I had a serious problem with drugs, but refused to really acknowledge the extent of it. I mean, I was diagnosed with gout (sudden, severe attacks of pain, redness, and tenderness in joints) at the age of twenty-three, due to how heavily I was drinking. That probably should have been a huge red flag, but like any good addict I just buried my head in the drugs and ignored it.

While in detox, where drugs weren't an option (at least for those five days), I finally had the opportunity to take a look at what my life had become, and it wasn't pretty. I experienced a very deep feeling of fear and depression, and there were no drugs to mask it (other than the benzos they had me on for withdrawals), so I was forced to sit with it, and it hurt. Physically, mentally, spiritually, and emotionally—it fucking hurt.

Being with myself for those five days allowed me to recognize that I didn't want to continue living the way I had been. In my heart, I knew that I'd wanted to stop for quite some time, but didn't know how; and here was my chance. From detox, I went to a twenty-eight-day inpatient treatment program, followed by two months in a halfway house. I was sober and recovering for a little over a year, but this isn't a pretty fairy tale, and I didn't go on to live happily ever after. I eventually relapsed, which became a pretty consistent pattern for me over the next few years—get sober, relapse, detox, rehab, repeat. With each cycle, however, it got worse. And my belief in my ability to heal continually diminished.

During that first year of sobriety, however, before relapsing, I felt compelled to finally set out on a search for something more. I engulfed myself in a completely no-bullshit exploration of spirituality. I found that having a deeply ingrained *question everything* punk-rock mind-set, which taught me not to accept everything at face value, allowed me to take a brutally honest look at the teachings of the various spiritual and religious paths I was exploring. Some of them hit me directly in my heart, while others left me scratching my head and wondering, "What the fuck?" Regardless of whether a particular teaching resonated with me or not, however, I always remembered a simple teaching that my mother blessed me with as a child, which was, "to each their own." So with that in mind, I found myself able to respect others who were finding their answers in methods and teachings that didn't resonate with me. It's an important theme in this book—*acceptance.*

In between relapses, during my times of sobriety, I would visit various sanghas, churches, temples, and other spiritual and religious institutions, and I remember noticing something that definitely surprised me, which was the increasing number of practitioners who shared many of the same eclectic spiritual and non-spiritual interests that I did. It was awesome to share time in meditation and discussing the teachings of the Buddha and Jesus, Lao Tzu and Krishna, but also spending time nerding out over movies like *The Big Lebowski* and *Donnie Darko*, and bands like Foo Fighters, A Tribe Called Quest, and Mastodon. One minute we'd be discussing Arjuna's internal struggle in the Bhagavad Gita, and the next we'd be laughing over shows like *Curb Your Enthusiasm* and *Arrested Development.* It was at this point I realized that the dogma and rigidity that had turned me off to religion and spirituality for the majority of my life weren't all there was to it, and that maybe I could get into this spirituality thing.

The experience of relating to people both on a spiritual and everyday human level—where it was okay to not be perfect, and even to laugh at our imperfections—was amazing. It was through interacting with those lighthearted and open-minded folks, and our shared eclectic interests, that I was inspired to search online for magazines or websites, in the hopes of connecting with more of these compassionate and quirky people I'd been getting to know. I thought there would have to be **in the spirit** places that celebrated both spirituality **of DIY ethics** and the other eclectic interests my new friends and I had been discussing, but my search was to no avail. So in the spirit of DIY ethics, I started a website called The Indie

Spiritualist, with the intention of creating an outlet for other seekers such as myself.

So, what is an indie spiritualist, and why does it matter? An indie spiritualist is more than someone who thinks independently or craves a spiritual path outside the traditional confines of religion. An indie spiritualist is someone who honors the spiritual truth within themselves, regardless of what popular society, religious institutions, friends, family, or anyone else, for that matter, prefer they think. The indie spiritualist stays true to the heart, because that's the most authentic teacher any of us will ever have. When we honor that internal nudge that tells us everything may not be exactly as it seems, and when we explore all that we've been told is true by society with the understanding that maybe it's not, we're taking our first steps toward awakening.

This book is a new introspective exercise in dogma-free, everyday spirituality that I hope will benefit seekers from all walks of life, whether you are new to the spiritual path or a longtime practitioner.

INTRODUCTION: SMASH THE
Control Machine

When we blindly adopt a religion,
a political system, a literary dogma,
we become automatons.
We cease to grow.

Anaïs Nin

Spirituality is often of little interest to those of us who are independent thinkers and don't necessarily feel like we fit in to mainstream cultural norms in terms of interests, passions, values, or attitudes. Whether we're a teenager, a twenty- or thirty-something or older; into punk rock, hip-hop, or alternative music; covered in tattoos and piercings; a skateboarder; gay, lesbian, bisexual, or transgender; a nerd; or even wearing a suit and tie—something *inside* of us has felt other than.

Many of us looked to religion or spirituality for answers, but soon found that neither the dogma of old religion nor the "love and light" fluffiness of New Age spirituality were approaches that resonated with us. Still, we were left with an internal yearning—one of virtually deafening silence—that compelled us to answer its call, but how? What can we do? What about the rest of us who don't resonate with the exceedingly positive love-and-light movement or the dogmatic tenets of spiritual and religious traditions? What are we left to do when we're looking for something more, something we can embrace exactly as we are?

At its core, spirituality is amazing. There have been many illumined teachers (both past and present) who have deeply affected me and many other indie-spirited people in very real and inspiring ways. However, as with anything in life, there's also no shortage of bullshit that can come along with spirituality. There are so many elements that can easily turn off any free-thinking individual, including, but not limited to, the self-proclaimed gurus, "enlightened" teachers who demand complete obedience of their students, yoga instructors who actually buy in to their students' worship of them, outrageously priced "spiritual" clothing and accessories, the stay-positive-at-all-costs rhetoric, and on and on it goes.

Though years of dogmatic attachments, rigid instructions, and fear-based campaigns have left many of us with not the fondest outlook on religion and spirituality, times are changing, and we no longer have to accept or allow our beliefs, or what resonates for us as truth, to be dictated by others.

For years I wrestled with how to reconcile my desire to walk a spiritual path, my love of independent culture, and my struggles with addiction and recovery. This ultimately led me to reevaluate everything in my life and to ask myself questions that are not typically discussed in spiritual circles. The ideas and questions were not overly esoteric. Rather, they were simple, introspective questions that I personally needed to work through in order to get a clearer picture of my path and purpose. (And as mentioned, this quest led me to create The Indie Spiritualist website.)

My spiritual awakening didn't happen on the mountaintops of the Himalayas or the ashrams of India. Nor did I find it in a church or monastery. Hell, I wasn't even looking for it in the first place, but spirituality can have a funny way of creeping into our lives, no matter how much of a protective barrier we set up.

Indie spiritualism is a new approach to divine experience for those who reject the trappings and hypocrisies of mainstream spirituality and organized religion, who feel a sense of otherness, and don't necessarily resonate with mainstream cultural norms. To quote William S. Burroughs: "Smash the control images. Smash the control machine." This saying has become somewhat of a template for most of the significant change in my life.

When it all comes down to it, living spiritually is a completely inside job. We don't need to change our appearance, adopt a new language, or change our mannerisms to fit in. We don't need to completely write spirituality off because we may be holding to our own stereotypes, and possibly miss out on some incredible insights and teachings that could make a difference in our lives. Dogma-free spirituality is just that: dogma free. You're free and open to the exploration.

My sincere and humble intention is that, in all your uniqueness, you find peace and happiness while being "you" and walking your own authentic spiritual path.

The following essays, vignettes, musings, and other writings are merely an exercise in dogma-free, everyday spirituality, which I hope will benefit seekers from all walks of life. It's not only my story, but, I believe, a story shared by many of us as we reconcile living an independent lifestyle with walking an authentic spiritual path.

living spiritually is a completely inside job

After the collection of vignettes is a "Side-B," which extends the invitation for those independent spiritual seekers who are interested in learning more about incorporating meditations and practices into their lives. These practices are from a wide spectrum of spiritual traditions and have been enormously helpful in my life.

Included at the end are some "Bonus Tracks," an eclectic list of personally recommended books, music, and films that may provide sources of inspiration in obvious as well as unconventional ways. Embedded throughout the book are QR codes—the first two of which are below—that you can use to read and listen to extra media content: links to some of my music, videos, and full interviews of the many individuals in the world who lent their voices and insight to the core of this work.

Noah Levine was not only generous enough to write the foreword for my book, but he gave me an interview. Here's a link to our talk, which aired on Where Is My Guru radio show.
http://www.whereismyguru.com/radio-show/susainable-living-dharma-punx-scott-pittman-noah-levine-mar-292013/

 As we start the book, I'd like to set the mood with a little music, about which I'm very passionate, as you can probably already tell based on the preface. The first song I'd like to share is "Invocation" by my band, Womb of the Desert Sun, from our EP Invocation: Our Dying Days.
http://www.beyondword.com/indiespiritualist/audiodownload1.m4a

Side A

ANGELS OF DARKNESS

(The Words, The Ways)

1

SPIRITUALITY?

The true word of God is written in our heart.

KRS-One, "Ain't Ready"

In a recent conversation with one of my friends, who was helping me take some pictures for my website's bio page, she playfully cracked on my interest in spirituality by teasing me that I wasn't smiling enough in the photos, and said, "What would all of the spiritual people think?" Her joke didn't mean much to me at the time, but later I really began to ponder why I was drawn to spirituality while she wasn't, and how her playful comment about "spiritual people" actually said a lot more than I had initially realized.

My friend and I are similar in many respects. We have a lot of tattoos, love independent culture, and look for more than what life has to offer at face value. When it comes to spirituality, however, she has little to no interest, and, after really thinking about a lot of what passes for spirituality these days, I honestly can't say that I blame her. It's hard for many of us to connect with popular and fashionable spirituality, especially since being popular and fashionable isn't of much importance to us to begin with. This scenario creates a problem, especially for the younger generations, who are looking for something more; and if, or when, we eventually turn to spirituality, our interests are quickly thwarted at the plasticity of what we find.

I mean absolutely no disrespect by addressing the way some teachers present spiritual material. Many of them do an excellent job of offering the material in a way that makes it easily accessible for popular society, especially here in the west. In fact, I'm friends with many of these teachers and I completely honor and respect their styles. However, just as some find that they resonate with Buddhism over Christianity, or vice versa, the same goes for today's spiritual aspirants who are looking for nontraditional spiritual and religious paths, but just can't find it in the pretty love-and-light circles.

Making spirituality accessible to all seekers, from all walks of life, is of paramount importance. This is because, unfortunately, those who are searching for something more, yet don't feel like they fit in with particular spiritual and religious groups, will instead often resort to material items such as drugs, shopping, food, sex, and so forth. In a less harmful, but just as fleeting way, some people seek acceptance and belonging by transforming their physical appearance via tanning, tattoos, piercings, plastic surgery, or expensive clothes. But these are all temporary things that will only fill the gap for so long.

There's absolutely nothing wrong with any of the aforementioned things—I'm personally covered in tattoos—but it's important to remember that things such as those are nothing more than material pleasures that won't transform us on a deeper, inner level. If that's what we're looking to do, we need to begin making over our insides instead.

Things came to a head for me some years ago when I was at a breaking point in my life. Years of active drug and alcohol addiction had left me at a place where I was going to either kill myself or find a better way to live. It was a dark time for me, but one that proved to be the catalyst that pushed me to find a more integrally healthy lifestyle. People like my photographer friend, however, who aren't at the edge of death or insanity, or backed into a corner like I was, often don't feel compelled to seek out deeper meanings from life. If they do, and they happen to look for it in much of today's contemporary spirituality, it's often not long before they remember why they hadn't looked there in the first place.

Talk of fire and brimstone, or the idea of giving up material possessions or living in caves and so forth, is typically not the average person's idea of a good time. But until recently, that's often what's been associated with spiritual practice. Conversely, much of today's spirituality has become fluffy and watered down, relying on things like quick-fix "Top Ten" lists that rarely, if ever, truly offer the seeker any lasting results. I recently heard a Buddhist monk reference this type of spirituality as "fast food for our minds." Besides being humorous, he was right.

spirituality has become fluffy and watered down

Much of today's spirituality has become a business, and business is good. But for people like my friend, and many others, who can see through bullshit a mile away, much of today's spirituality just doesn't do it for them. I mean, some of the things that pass for spirituality these days could almost be humorous, if it wasn't so sad. And the price tags attached to much of it . . . well, like I said, business is good.

So much of this so-called spirituality is presented as pretty and cosmetic, and basically is to spirituality what *Jersey Shore* is to reality. Even when unsavory things—like our judging minds and low self-esteem—are addressed, they're given fun, kitschy names or catch phrases to put a shiny spin on them. So much of it only addresses the happy and positive aspects, focusing on words like "empowering" and "healing." But if people aren't scratching below the surface to those areas where the real healing and empowerment can come from—the darker places we'd rather pretend weren't there—then how deep and long lasting will said empowerment and healing actually be?

As for myself, I want to really lay it all out there, both the good and the bad. Life can be brutally ugly and grotesque, and I don't want to pretend otherwise. As much as we like to ignore the things that scare us, like the fact that death is always creeping up on us, what good does it do to deny life's ugliness? I mean, I hate to be the bearer of bad news, but at this very moment, you and I, we're dying.

Of course, it's important to celebrate life and love, friends and family, and I'm not trying to come across in a morbid way. Rather, I acknowledge and recognize that, for most of us, there's some scary shit we've become complacent in ignoring. Once we muster the courage to look our physical mortality in the face, though, we open ourselves to a deeper relationship with our true Self.

True spirituality embraces all of this: the beauty that is almost too much to bear, as well as the pain that leads some to the brink of insanity. It's all grist for the mill. We practice our asanas and mantras, prayers and aspirations, and that's great; but are they serving to strengthen our identity as a "spiritual person" or to help us release our identification with that illusion, and in the process deepen our exploration of more than meets the eye?

I'm not perfect. I'm so far from it, it's ridiculous, and I want to be absolutely clear on that. At times I fail at much of what I write about. I buy in to mental labels of myself and others, and get caught up in material shit. Here's a little story to help illustrate this point: Before writing this, I was packing up my drums, as I'm scheduled to play kirtan later on at Kripalu, a well-known Yoga retreat center here in the Northeast. When I finished packing the drums, I grabbed my Saucony sneakers, but noticed my pair of Vans sitting right next to them.

The quandary was that the Sauconys are made from suede, while the Vans are made from canvas. So I stopped for a minute and thought about how I was going to be performing in front of a bunch of yoga practitioners, and well, hmm, what would they think if I were wearing suede shoes? So yeah, that's the level I was recently coming from. But I'll just keep on keepin' on and do my best to bring awareness and compassion to the ridiculousness that is Chris Grosso, and to not take it all so goddamn seriously.*

---

* P.S. I wore the Sauconys. Namaste.

2

WHATEVER COMES UP,
Comes Out

It is not for me to judge another man's life.
I must judge, I must choose,
I must spurn, purely for myself.
For myself, alone.

Hermann Hesse, Siddhartha

I struggled with even addressing this topic at first. But since I've caught shit for it before, via feedback on articles I've written for various eco/spiritual websites, I'm sure I'll get even more disapproval for also doing so in this book. The fact is . . . I swear. Yup, I'm uncouth and at times have the mouth of a sailor, yet I still write about spiritual topics. Go figure.

I'll admit that at times I incorporate the word "fuck" into some of my articles usually for no other reason than to shake things up a bit. But, I mean, that can't really be any more harmful than, say, Chögyam Trungpa Rinpoche, the renowned and celebrated Buddhist scholar, teacher, and poet, whose wild escapades included sex scandals, drinking sake while giving lectures, and more. None of that, however, at least in my opinion, can take away from the brilliance of what he taught, which has guided countless spiritual seekers to a place of great meaning and liberation in their lives.

Watching the way that some people react to Rinpoche's lifestyle—or, on a smaller scale, to silly little swear words in spiritual articles—has taught me that it really has nothing to do with Rinpoche nor myself (not that I think I'm in any way near the level Rinpoche was). It's one's own personal attachments and inhibitions around words and lifestyles that make them uncomfortable, so I've learned to never take it personally. I would, however, sincerely urge those who are easily offended by such trivial things to really explore why that is rather than just chalking it up to living in accordance with societal or, even worse, "spiritual" standards.

I began writing this piece last night, almost begrudging the fact that such a topic needed to be addressed in the first place, but I did it anyway. As I went to sleep, I reconciled it by reminding myself that I kept it under five hundred words, so it would only be a very minor portion of this book. However, at 4:00 AM, something happened that would bring full circle the realization of just how truly unimportant this topic is.

I woke up abruptly to the sound of blaring sirens racing down my short, dead-end street. I sat up in my bed and immediately saw a huge ball of orange glowing through the trees. Putting on my glasses, I could see that it was my neighbors' house, engulfed in flames. I threw on a pair of shorts and a hoodie, walked down the street, and watched as their entire material existence went up in flames before my very own eyes—and theirs. Thankfully, they got out OK, though sadly their dog did not.

As I sit here a few hours later, finishing this piece, our street is still closed and I can hear the sounds of firemen sifting through the wreckage of my neighbors' home, which has been reduced to nothing more than a hollowed-out image of the life they once knew.

Things like that fire happen daily, often to families who are not as lucky to make it out alive. And on a larger scale, there are tragedies occurring worldwide on a daily—no, an hourly—basis: rape, murder, terrorism, natural disasters, hate crimes, and so much more. All things that, for me, put in clear-as-day perspective just how truly ridiculous it is to even have to have a conversation about swearing and spirituality in the first place.

3

SAMADHI AND VAN HALEN

*Mind is consciousness which has put on limitations.
You are originally unlimited and perfect.
Later you take on limitations and become the mind.*

Ramana Maharshi

Most people wouldn't associate profound spiritual experiences with the band Van Halen, and prior to the experience I'm about to share with you, neither would have I. However, it's a perfect example of how, when we have preconceived notions about how spirituality is supposed to be, we may very well be missing out on some amazing things!

It was roughly seven years ago that my brother and I had free tickets to see Van Halen play the Mohegan Sun Arena in Uncasville, Connecticut. I grew up enjoying Van Halen (not Van Hagar, though, fine, they did some good stuff too) and thought it'd be a cool nostalgic experience to go see them, especially since they'd just reunited with David Lee Roth (yes, again). All in all, they put on a hell of a show, but my personal highlight was an epic twenty-minute guitar solo by Eddie Van Halen.

It was toward the middle of Van Halen's set that Eddie began his solo while the other band members proceeded off stage. As I stood there watching EVH shred, his playing intensified, to the point where I found myself literally mesmerized by it. There was nothing else happening in my reality except his fingers moving on the neck of his guitar and the sounds they subsequently produced.

It was one of the most real moments of *samadhi* (a state of intense concentration achieved through dedicated meditation) I've ever experienced, which all came to a head around the fifteen-minute mark of Eddie's solo. I stood there, completely lost in the experience, until I found myself abruptly snapping out of it as I began to fall into the row of seats in front of me. I'd lost myself so deeply in the music that my body proceeded to act accordingly by completely letting itself go. Luckily, I caught myself before I fell down or knocked anyone over. In embarrassed amazement, I watched EVH finish his solo before the rest of the band joined him on stage and went into their next song. Oh, and I was completely sober during this experience, by the way.

Trust me when I tell you I'm not exaggerating this experience at all. One of the coolest things about it was the fact that I'm not even the biggest Van Halen fan and would have never in a million years seen this experience coming. Of course, Van Halen rocks and they are an amazing band, but if I was going to have an experience like this, I'd personally have expected it to happen while seeing a band like Sigur Rós or Explosions in the Sky, whose ambient music easily puts me into a meditative

Sigur Rós or Explosions in the Sky

state. The experience, however, was a perfect example of how, when we're open-minded and in touch with spirituality, amazing things can happen anytime and anywhere!

To be at a rock concert, of all places, with the crowd going crazy and music blaring, but still experience a transcendental state, a place where the awareness of even myself subsided and all that was left were the notes of EVH's guitar—yeah, I'd say you could call that spiritual.

4

THE ZIPPER THAT BROKE
the Camel's Tooth

Pucker up and kiss the asphalt now

At The Drive-In, "One Armed Scissor"

When I awoke that first morning at the rehab facility in
New Jersey—the one I'd be spending the next two months
at—my head throbbed. I imagine the pain would be borderline
unbearable for most, but, as those of us with the disease of addiction
know, our tolerance for pain typically exceeds that of the average
person (and please don't take this as bragging, because in actuality
it's really quite sad that our lives have brought us to such hellacious
internal and external places).

The amount of emotional, physical, spiritual, and mental pain we
subject ourselves to and tolerate is baffling at best, and my condition
when I awoke that morning was no exception. With panic attacks,
sweat, diarrhea, headache, nausea, disorientation, and very little
memory of my travels from Connecticut to New Jersey, I felt . . . well,
actually really quite normal, which is obviously pretty fucked up.

A clinical assistant informed me that I'd pissed myself the night
before, and threw a pair of bright white shorts on the floor. The
shorts had been left behind by a previous client, and I needed them
not only because I'd pissed myself, but also because either I or the bus

line had managed to lose my luggage at the layover stop in New York. I was so out of my mind, however, that to this day I don't remember changing buses, nor do I know who was actually responsible for losing my luggage, which contained all of my clothes and toiletries. (If I were to take a guess as to who was at fault, however, I'd say it was the guy who was drunk enough to make even Bukowski nod his head in respect.)

After trying on the shorts provided, I found that not only were they something I'd normally definitely not wear (style- and color-wise), but they were also one size too small. So I decided that, rather than dealing with the discomfort of their tightness all day, I'd instead wear my piss-soaked shorts to group. I mean, they were only slightly damp at that point, and the odor was surprisingly minimal. Well, at least to me it was, possibly because I was still totally out of my mind.

That first day of group was hell, and the anxiety and nausea only seemed to intensify as morning turned into afternoon. For each of the group sessions, I found a seat as far back and tucked away as I could. When lunchtime arrived, I made my way over to the building where food was served, but couldn't stomach anything.

That first day of group was hell

I did, coincidentally, run into another person I'd been in detox with back in Connecticut prior to leaving for New Jersey (he'd arrived in New Jersey about two days before I had) and while it was nice to see a familiar face, I definitely wasn't in the mood for talking. The only thing I remember him saying to me was something like, "Man, you reek of alcohol. Were you drinking this morning?" While it'd been over twelve hours since my last drink, I'm sure the scent of extremely cheap vodka not only permeated my breath but seeped through my pores as well—but who knows, maybe that helped mask the odor of my piss-stained shorts.

After group session ended for the day, there was a two-hour window before the other clients and I were to leave for a twelve-step meeting. I took that time to bury myself under the covers of my bed.

As much as I wanted to escape the agony of my current mental and physical state by falling asleep, the overwhelming anxiety and panic I was experiencing wouldn't allow it. Before I knew it, I found myself piling into a van with the other residents, heading out to the meeting.

My only memory from that evening at the meeting is sitting in a cold room with the air conditioning blasting, yet still sweating profusely from the overwhelming anxiety and nausea I was experiencing. After the meeting, the evening clinician on duty saw the state I was in and proceeded to read my file. She learned that I had a history of seizures due to withdrawals, and, after conferring with the evening nurse, decided to put me on a benzodiazepine taper to prevent the possibility of a seizure.

While the benzo settled my stomach a bit, it did little more than mask the anxiety I was experiencing, so I was still unable to sleep at all that night. The next morning, as I was getting ready for group, I decided it best not to push my luck with the piss-soaked shorts again, and put on the one-size-too-small pair of whiter-than-white shorts I'd been given.

That morning, I was given another benzo, which only added to my already exceedingly tired state, and it wasn't long before I found myself nodding off during the first group. Halfway through, I was called over to the adjacent building to meet with another of the facility's nurses, who wanted to check my vitals and see how I was doing overall, as she'd read the note the nurse had written about my condition the night before.

As I waited, I had to pee, so I made my way to a bathroom at the end of the hall. I was so tired that I found myself sitting down to go, and it was after I finished, standing in a sort of half-hunched way, that I zipped up those ridiculously uncomfortable shorts, and the zipper broke.

I remember mumbling out loud to myself, "Are you fucking serious?!" before proceeding to bend over and pick the zipper up from off the floor. While examining the zipper in my zombie-esque state, I noticed that a part of the metal binding had slipped out of place. It looked as though I'd be able to bend it back in place if I could just open a piece of the zipper latch enough to make room for it to slide in.

The piece was too small for my sweaty fingers to bend, so I decided that the most sensible thing to do would be to use my teeth. Well, about two seconds into my attempt, I heard a cracking sound and proceeded to watch a considerable piece of my tooth fall onto the floor.

And so it was with that zipper/tooth incident that my mind went blank and my body slowly slunk itself to the ground, shorts still around my knees. I remember sort of mentally laughing to myself. It wasn't a humorous laugh, but rather a laugh of insanity. I felt like I wanted to cry, but I'd been so detached from feeling for so long that I just couldn't. "This is what my life has become," I thought to myself, and continued to just sit there in a bewildered state of depression and self-loathing.

It wasn't until the nurse eventually came and knocked on the door that I stood up, pulled the shorts up to my waist, and went about the rest of my day. Internally, I was as broken as that zipper.

I'm the type of person who's typically pretty good at hiding his emotions, but there was no hiding my overwhelming experience of pain and depression at that point. Those shorts and the broken zipper obviously weren't such a big deal in the scope of real life issues; but, for me, at that time and in my condition, they were much more than just shorts and a zipper. They were a symbolic representation of what my life had become, which was uncomfortably tight, broken, and bright-ass white.

I was fucking shot, lost, done, completely over all of it, and didn't care who knew it. All the various spiritual books I'd read at that point, and all the various practices I'd endeavored upon, they meant shit to me; everything meant shit to me.

"Places That Scare You" by Chris Grosso.
http://www.beyondword.com/indiespiritualist/
audiodownload2.m4a

5

DETOX DIARIES

This is what hell looks like when all the fires are burned.
Cable, "Running Out of Roads to Ride"

"**N**o mud, no lotus." It's a saying I've held close to my heart for the greater part of the last decade as I've fumbled my way through the addiction/recovery process. I'm grateful that more of those ten years have been spent sober and recovering than in active addiction. However, there has been no shortage of return visits to the mud that gives birth to lilies in the first place.

While I still have trouble considering myself a writer, in retrospect, I've always had a propensity for writing, based on the stacks of journals I've kept tucked away in my closet from years gone by. The thing is, the majority of those journals are filled with the dark times.

The pages are littered with writings penned during my years in active addiction as well as my various trips to detox and rehab. Occasionally, I'll sift through those pages to remind myself how I used to live, as a sobering reminder that I can end up right back there (best-case scenario) if I don't keep myself in check.

It can be a painful experience, reading the hopeless sentiment held within the majority of those words, but one that, in the end, also reminds me of the limitless power of hope, which I know beyond a shadow of a doubt is the underlying reason why I'm still alive today.

When I revisit those journals' pages of depression and despair, I find I'm often most affected by the words I wrote while I was in detox. I think that's because those were the times my head started to feel some semblance of clarity after what had surely been weeks, if not months, of an unbearably painful relapse experience.

I say "some semblance of clarity" because, in detox, I was still under the influence of benzodiazepines, which sort of helps with the pain of withdrawals, but, more importantly, helps keep seizures from occurring in the process. However, they were controlled doses administered by nurses, which was a huge step toward mental clarity compared to the insane amounts of drugs and alcohol I'd been ingesting leading up to that.

I didn't have the capacity to keep up any sort of facade

While in detox, I would find myself in a mental, emotional, spiritual, and physical place that was extremely raw, vulnerable, depressed, and surprisingly open. Open in the sense that I was so tired and so broken that I didn't have the capacity to keep up any sort of facade, which resulted in some of the most honest, albeit still chemically influenced, writing from the darkest places in my life.

The following four pieces are just a very small sample of the mental places I was in during those dark times. These are the pieces my editors felt were applicable for this book. But in the interest of full disclosure, they definitely don't reflect the truest depths of how hopeless and dark things got for me. However, I understand that there is truly no need to share the darkest of the dark writings—the suicidal ideations and so forth—because the following still offers an intimate look into my experience while sparing you the most graphic details.

Most importantly, the following pieces are shared in the hope that, as you read them, you come to understand that no matter how dark things got for me, I still found my way back, which means I know with my entire essence of being that, no matter what you've been through, or how lost you may find yourself right now, you can absolutely find your way back too.

Undead

Fuck. Detox again. I'm trying to let go and remember I am in this dark place for a reason, but to no avail. It may sound crazy, but I can sense the demons all around. In the corners, under the beds, crawling on the ceilings, *everywhere*. I don't know where the angels are, though. Perhaps once the ambulance stretcher hits that front door, they're not allowed in. This place is just so dark and cold and littered with living zombies. It's as if I can actually see tombstones in some of their eyes. The dates may be blurry, but the tombstones are there nevertheless. I wonder if these zombies see the same in my eyes too. I wonder if I'm even seen in the first place. And the scariest thing down here is that there are shadows in places where they shouldn't be.

Toilet Bowl Spirituality

It feels as if the closer I come to giving up, the more the bits and pieces make sense. Brain waves, central nervous system, neurotransmitters, and all the finite subtleties make this whole thing seem real, but Ramana Maharshi laid it out so simply for us. I am not my body, thoughts, or organs, and yet, at the same time, I am all of it—the dual housed within the nondual. It seems as if it all comes together so we can witness it, witness God, witness the beauty, the pain, the senselessness of it all. But then what? Life is more than the traditional illusion most people are conditioned to buy in to, but shit, I can't blame them for buying into it. Hell, I wish I was them, buying into it myself, sometimes. So where does that leave us/me? I say "us/me" because I'm tired of writing as if I actually believe in the illusion of you and I. For example, the vomit that leaves my mouth as I endure these withdrawals, ending up in a toilet bowl, sink, or even the floor, is also us. We're vomiting into ourselves. Now *there* is spirituality. Everything coming full circle, no matter how messy, gross, or confusing it may be. Fucking life is beautiful and disgusting and that's just the reality of it.

Soul Decay

The cuts on my wrists are making it hard to write right now, but I want to say this—detox truly is you against you. It's not like there's anyone here encouraging you; there's no one here to say, "Hey, nice job detoxing" or any shit like that. It's literally just you experiencing the hell of the drugs leaving your body. And while the heavily medicated state in which detox leaves you helps mask some of the pain, there's no medication that can stop you from feeling parts of your soul decaying . . . and that's fucking tough.

A Pen and Some Paper

I gummed my meds last night and this morning (hid them between my teeth and lip in order to spit them out rather than swallow them), because I'm tired of not feeling. So I'm a bit more coherent as I write this. And it's in this coherence that I'm realizing this community room smells terrible. It's like a mixture of moldy furniture and unbathed humans. I'm fucking bored. I think "miserable" would also be a fair, descriptive word to use. I'm hoping to get out of here today. This morning they had us do an activity with Play-Doh. I'm fucking serious, actual Play-Doh, so yeah, really hoping to get the fuck out of here today. It's sad, but I'm just realizing a smile hasn't crossed this face in a long time. I'm not looking for sympathy, and you can call me a pussy all you want. It's just that I've realized I'm nothing more than a broken man with a pen and some paper.

"The Complete Fiction" by Chris Grosso.
http://www.beyondword.com/indiespiritualist/
audiodownload3.m4a

6

THE GIFT OF DESPERATION

And I know this ghost
I have seen it before

Converge, "The Saddest Day"

In retrospect, I can now see that life was hitting me over the head with a metaphoric sledgehammer in order to realign me with the course *it* had intended—since I obviously wasn't willing to pay attention of my own accord. I was blessed with what the twelve-step fellowships call the "gift of desperation," which means that I'd hit such a rock bottom and that I was finally able to surrender. I had nothing left to hold on to, and nothing holding me back. I was completely bankrupt in every sense of the word—morally, spiritually, emotionally, and physically—which allowed me to completely let go. In turn, letting go allowed for true inner spiritual growth to begin.

I try daily to rest in gratitude, knowing that, while I'll be an addict for the rest of my life, I no longer have to live the scumbag way that I used to. I somehow managed to live through that experience, which is not the case for so many others, and that fact is not lost on me. I think not only about the pain that I caused my loved ones, but the collective pain that is experienced by *all* loved ones who are affected by addictions of any kind. It's with that thought that I hold the aspiration of love and healing for them all in my heart.

The pain and sorrow I experience from my past actions is almost overwhelming when I sit in presence with it, but it is also a catalyst that constantly inspires me to keep moving forward, making a daily amends through my actions and helping others in gratitude however I can.

I'm living a different way of life today, a life that is by no means perfect, nor always filled with happiness, but a life that is filled with a deeper sense of calm, serenity, integrity, and conscious contact with the Universal love that is far beyond what my limited vocabulary could ever begin to describe. And so I say . . . Fuck skeletons. Fuck closets. I'm offering this, the good, bad, beautiful, ugly—all of it— with the awareness that, in this moment, it is all exactly as it is, and it is imperfectly perfect.

"Drawing Static" by Chris Grosso.
http://www.beyondword.com/indiespiritualist/
audiodownload4.m4a

7

FINDING FREEDOM

*Only to the extent that we expose ourselves
over and over to annihilation can that which is
indestructible in us be found.*

Pema Chödrön

A few days into rehab, I met with one of the facility's clinical directors. Welcoming me into his office, he noticed a Medicine Buddha tattoo on the back of my leg. (A Medicine Buddha is believed to cure all suffering through his teachings, or "medicine"; obviously, I hadn't been paying close enough attention to what he was saying.) Having his own interest in Buddhism, the clinical director and I proceeded to spend the next twenty minutes discussing its various tenets, as well as spirituality in general.

Then he told me about a book called *Finding Freedom*, by San Quentin death-row inmate Jarvis Jay Masters. While I wasn't familiar with the book, I recognized Jarvis's name; author and Buddhist nun Pema Chödrön had mentioned him in some of her audio talks I'd listened to. The director told me a bit about the book and how Masters found Buddhism while living on death row, ultimately leading to his own personal redemption. He also told me he'd bring in his copy for me to borrow and read.

I was all for it. I've always loved the revolutionary type of writing from people like Mumia Abu-Jamal, Huey Newton, Eldridge

Cleaver, Leonard Peltier, and so forth, but with *Finding Freedom*'s added element of spirituality, I found myself actually looking forward to something for the first time in quite a while.

As I began to read *Finding Freedom*, I knew within the first few pages that it was no accident that the book had found its way to me in my darkest hours of despair. As I read through its stories, my reactions ranged from complete shock to sincere laughter—with the most important part of the experience, however, being centered on the hope I took away from everything Jarvis had to say.

I mean, here was a death-row inmate, housed in one of America's most notoriously violent penitentiaries—San Quentin State Prison— living in rat- and shit-infested conditions with violence as the audio and visual soundtrack of his daily life. Yet, he still found the resolve within himself to completely renounce his own violent past and selfish ways, and, in turn, commit his life to the benefit of all beings.

The book had a deep impact on me, not necessarily because there was a relation between his prison life and my own experience with addiction (though it would be fair to say that addiction is a state of imprisonment all its own), but because of the fact that he found hope in the most hopeless place possible: death row. In Jarvis's stories, I found inspiration from a man who himself found redemption and healing. I knew if Jarvis could do it there on death row, I could definitely do it myself in a comparatively cushier situation such as rehab.

As I took the first steps toward finding my own freedom, I began to look at the wreckage of my recent past in a fearless and uncompromising way. This was fucking terrifying, to say the least, but it was the fear that was keeping me stuck exactly where I was, and that was a truly awful place to be. So I had a choice to make: I could either do my time in rehab only to leave and go back to drinking myself to death—or, I could find the resolve I knew I had in my heart to pick myself back up and make the necessary changes in my life, no matter how difficult the process might be. Jarvis's stories helped me believe that, if he could do it, then so could I. And so I did.

I also made another little vow of my own while in rehab, which was to do whatever I could to help spread the word about Jarvis, and

I kept true to that after I got out. I checked out the website listed in his book, freejarvis.org, and sent an email with my request to coordinate an interview with him over the phone at San Quentin, to publish on my website in an effort to help spread the word about his case. After a few days, I received an email from Jarvis's wonderful wife, who said she would talk to him about the request, and it was shortly thereafter that I heard back from her, letting me know that he was on board for the interview.

And so it was over the course of roughly a month, and ten phone calls, that I got to speak with, and know in an even more intimate way, the man who'd had such an impact on me and my life. Jarvis and I spoke about many different things, ranging from Buddhism to addiction, the Sandy Hook Elementary School shootings, his life on death row, and much more.

Jarvis supplied me with a plethora of wisdom and shared just as candidly during our interview as he did in *Finding Freedom*. The following excerpt completely reiterates the experience I had of finding that hope deep down inside myself and honoring my will to live, thanks to Jarvis's inspiring words. I had to ask him to elaborate on how he makes peace with being in prison, especially since he's been imprisoned for over thirty years now, the majority of which has been for a crime he didn't even commit. Jarvis's response was

Well, I've been so blessed, man, and it's a weird thing that I don't even get sometimes. I mean, I've been here thirty-one years and wrote a book that's helped a lot of people. I think about how, if they released me five years after I initially got here in 1981, instead of how many people I've now helped, how many more people I could have hurt, how much more pain I could have inflicted . . . How can I say thirty-one years has been a total waste when, it hasn't.[1]

We talked about how important it is to be authentic with one's true nature, understanding that, as Jarvis says, "People in and of themselves are not necessarily bad . . . It's the bad things we do that reflect all the bullshit that's going on in people's lives . . . How we often wish our lives to be a whole lot different, but we come to find out that we wouldn't have that experience were it not for the troubles." The Buddhist publication Tricycle magazine even caught wind of the condensed interview I'd published on elephantjournal.com and wrote about it on their website.

 You can read the full version of my " Finding Freedom " interview with Jarvis Jay Masters on TheIndie-Spiritualist.com. http://theindiespiritualist.com/2013/01/29/finding-freedom-an-interview-with-author-buddhist-and-san-quentin-death-row-inmate-jarvis-jay-masters/.

So, in continuing to take Jarvis's inspiration to heart, I carried on with the unpleasant task of looking at what a shit show my life had become, as well as assessing the work that needed to be done in order to continue the healing process for both myself and others.

Often in the beginning stages of healing or recovery, most addicts, or abusers of any kind, find it extremely difficult to express even the slightest semblance of love toward themselves, and I was no exception. Taking into consideration the already existing condition of self-loathing that most addicts experience, and adding to that the countless shitty things we've done to ourselves and others while in our active addictive states—whether it was prostituting ourselves; physically, mentally, or emotionally harming ourselves or others; losing our wife, husband, or children; or any number of very difficult circumstances to face—it's obvious that the odds of learning to love ourselves are stacked against us from the very beginning.

With that being the case, what are we left to do? Personally, I found that the most beneficial thing I could do was to start by getting honest with myself, to tell the fucking truth. And I'm not talking about some "tiptoeing around whatever the situation or circumstance may be" half-truth, but a "full on, brutally honest exploration into self" truth.

In *Finding Freedom*, Jarvis wrote, "For a long time I had been my own stranger, but everything I went through in learning how to accept myself brought me to the doorsteps of dharma, the Buddhist path." We need not be Buddhist to appreciate his sentiment in those words. We all go through a ton of shit in our lives, and it's that shit which, as Jarvis says, makes us a stranger to ourselves. The question is, now that we're aware of that, what are we going to do with it?

For Jarvis, it led to the Buddhist path. For me, it was reconciliation with the desire to live life. How about you? What's your shit and how are you going to use it to make positive changes? You don't need to be an inmate or an addict to have experienced your own share of struggles in life, so this question really is applicable to anyone who reads it.

As I kept moving forward in my recovery, I began to explore the reasons I was so scared to look at the things that sucked in my life—self-loathing, fear, emotional scars, and other baggage. I began to see clearly the futile nature of the fear *behind the fear*. And herein lies a perfect opportunity to explore why we're scared to take an honest look at the unpleasant things in our life (besides the obvious fact that they're unpleasant). And more importantly, to figure out what we can do today to begin taking even small steps toward changing that.

I'm not trying to make this sound like an after-school special or some cheesy motivational type thing, but if we're really sick and tired of being sick and tired, well, then some shit has got to change. Other people can (and should) most definitely help us through this difficult process, but ultimately it's up to us to decide to even begin making the change in the first place.

Jarvis, while on death row, decided to completely change his life and begin practicing nonviolence and other acts to benefit the well-being of those both inside and out of prison.† Luckily for us, we don't

some shit has got to change

need to be on death row, or even have an interest in any particular religion or spirituality, to begin making significant changes in our lives for the better.

I'm not saying this is simply a matter of making the decision to change, and then everything magically becomes better, because that's a crock of shit. However, if we don't at least make the decision to change in the first place, we'll keep doing what we've always done, and, in turn, keep getting what we've always gotten.

After I personally made the decision to change, I knew there was work to be done. Like I said, I had to get honest with myself, brutally honest. I began to open up a little bit in the groups I was attending in rehab, though, for the most part, I still kept the majority of my internal mess held safely under lock and key.

I did, however, get myself a journal, and I began putting some of the heavier stuff to paper because I felt like, even though I couldn't trust anyone else with it yet, I still needed to begin getting some of it out. I knew there was still a lot of heavy stuff I wasn't ready to face, even in a journal, but I wrote what I could and began letting go what I was ready to.

I wrote about the deep sadness I felt due to all of the pain I'd caused my family throughout the years, and how unbearably sad it made me to think about all the times they saw me strapped down in emergency rooms because I was wasted out of my mind. I wrote about all the blackouts I'd experienced and the countless people I'd fucked over. I thought about the kids at the job I'd just lost due to my relapse, and how most of them would be lied to when they asked why I wasn't at work anymore.

As I continued to write, I found myself slowly beginning to open up a bit more in groups and became increasingly aware of a cathartic release I'd often feel afterward. I still felt a lot of guilt and shame around many of my actions, as well as plenty of residual self-loathing as a result, but I found that, as I allowed myself to be vulnerable with others about some of the things I'd done in the past, and how the pain I'd caused others wreaked havoc on my mental and emotional states, I realized I was not alone in my pain, just as *you* are not alone in yours either.

I began to see, out of the corners of my eyes (which were usually fixated on the floor while I would share), others nodding their heads, as if they too had experienced what I was talking about. In turn, I would feel some relief as I embraced the notion that others could relate and that I wasn't so alone in this.

After voluntarily completing two months of inpatient rehab treatment, I moved home with my parents. For the first time in my life, I had no job and found myself filing for unemployment. I had no idea what I was going to do. The one thing I had committed myself to, however, was living life.

 "All About Us" by Chris Grosso.
http://www.beyondword.com/indiespiritualist/
audiodownload5.m4a

---

† To learn more about Jarvis Jay Masters's case and how you can help, please visit freejarvis.org.

8

CALLING BULLSHIT ON OURSELVES

*The most terrifying thing is to
accept oneself completely.*

C. G. Jung

Man, am I good at putting on a front.

I'm guessing most of you, if you were really to take an honest look at yourselves, could probably relate. But, for the purposes of this piece, I'll take one for the team and completely throw myself under the bus.

Now, when I say "putting on a front," I'm talking about the *me* I let others see versus the *me* that's underneath that exterior, the guy pretty much no one knows. Whether we're conscious of it or not, we all have that *me*. The *me* that we show others, the one pretending to have their shit together, both externally as well as internally.

In my case, it's the guy who writes articles on spirituality and plays kirtan. He's peaceful and compassionate and understanding. And while, sure, there's definitely truth to that him, some of him is farce as well.

That *me*, the one I keep hidden away, well, he's scared to death of letting you see who he really is. He doesn't want you to know he's terrified of failure. He's great at **terrified of failure**

29

hiding the fact that he's completely insecure about his musical skills, and that he often struggles to feel like he really has anything of worth to say. Oh, and a personal favorite, he often gets wrapped up in feeling fat and gross after eating like shit for a day or two.

He usually spends his weekends at home alone—writing, creating music, reading, and maybe hitting up a twelve-step meeting. He's okay in his solitude—actually, he enjoys it, truth be told—but yeah, it's far from the exciting life others may think he leads.

He's there when I lay my head down at night and greets me when I rise from bed in the morning. His is the image I see reflecting back in the mirror as I brush my teeth and to whom I do my best to send loving-kindness, sometimes successfully, other times not.

Now, I don't want to paint the wrong picture here—he's not always full of shitty feelings and thoughts, or feeling insecure. He definitely experiences joy and peace and can be happy with things he's written or happy with the way a kirtan performance went and sometimes . . . sometimes he likes the physical image reflecting back at him in the mirror.

A part of him knows he helps others, and he feels gratitude when he receives emails from those who've read his stuff and were impacted by it. Overall, though, for whatever reason, he's terribly scared to let *you* see who he really is. It's through the recognition of this fear, however, that the opportunity arises for things to begin to change.

For now, I've come to understand and experience that, as humans, we have our built-in survival skills, and the desire to be accepted is definitely one of them. I also feel, however, that when it comes to being socially accepted and fitting others' standards in order to be embraced and accepted, that I should know better.

Why am I so scared to let you see the real me? After sitting with that question for a while, I struggled to come up with some insightful, epiphany-esque realization, and therein I found the answer. It's not that I care so much about fitting in socially and keeping my little demons to myself, per se. But rather, I realized that, since childhood, society has conditioned me to be fearful of embracing myself

unconditionally and allowing people to see me for who I am. And I
know I'm not alone; it's what many of us have known as far back as
we can remember. We're told to hide our emotions, be strong, and
don't rock the boat, and we listen, because it's usually from our parents, teachers, and friends. Of course they believe they have our best
interests in heart, and, in all fairness, they were only teaching us the
same things they were taught themselves growing up. It's a deeply
rooted thing, this desire to be accepted by others, and the fear of
being rejected—socially, physically, spiritually, and otherwise—is an
awful *fucking* fear.

Then there's the fear of facing ourselves for who we truly are:
the good, the bad, and the really, really ugly . . . and that too is an
awful *fucking* fear. But until we're willing to take a good hard look
at both of the selves we believe ourselves to be—the person we present to the world and the person we hide at all costs, who's rooted in
fear—well, we'll stay stuck exactly where we are.

You were born to be real, not to be perfect.

How humanity lost its connection to the root of our true essence,
which is *love*, may never be known. However, it's our inherent right
to take that love back. And I'm not talking about the fluffy love-and-
light kind of love, but rather the love that truly can't be spoken of or
explained (yeah, yeah, I know I'm trying to write about it right now,
but you get what I'm trying to say).

As I sat in meditation this morning before writing this, I
brought my attention to my heart center and mentally thanked God/
Universe/Spirit for being real, and for His/Her/Its Grace in my life.
I mean, I really sat with that and acknowledged it, and, as I was mentally saying those words, I knew God was there with me in real time,
hearing them.

A funny thing happened right after I
made that acknowledgement—my entire
body felt as though it were alive in a way
that was almost too much to handle. I felt
my cells dancing and my heart so full of
love it was as if it were going to explode.

an awful fucking fear

All of a sudden, tears began streaming from my eyes, tears of a *profound* gratitude.

I share that to say this: There are a number of methods that facilitate healing and self-acceptance. Teachers like Pema Chödrön, Gangaji, Thich Nhat Hanh, and countless others have written amazing books on doing just that. When we allow the *love* that is our true nature to guide us, whether it's through reading books by those authors, meditating, or whatever other practices we implement, we *cannot* fail.

Underground music icon Henry Rollins once said, "Scar tissue is stronger than regular tissue. Realize the strength, move on." I'm quite sure that we all have our fair share of scar tissue. With that being said, what better place to start than there, and what better time to start than, like, *right fucking now*?

9

NO COMPLY

*The search for reality is the most
dangerous of all undertakings,
for it will destroy the world in which you live.
But if your motive is love of truth and life,
you need not be afraid.*

Sri Nisargadatta Maharaj

The Indie Spiritualist website has provided me the chance to interview a lot of people who've significantly impacted me throughout my life and continue to help me open my eyes to new ways of seeing the world. Whether it's spiritual teachers such as Dan Millman or Robert Thurman, professional skateboarders such as Mike Vallely or Christian Hosoi, musicians like Deftones, Kaki King, or Aesop Rock, or even people from the world of film, such as director George A. Romero, Demetri Martin, and Danny Trejo—they've all helped and inspired me in one way or another in my life.

One person I felt particularly honored to interview was punk icon Ian MacKaye of Minor Threat and Fugazi. As I sat down to contemplate what I would ask Ian in our interview, I put on Fugazi's *Repeater* album to set the mood. Almost instantly, it took me back to the mid '90s, and I began daydreaming about the Connecticut clubs I frequented as a teenager—Studio 158, The Tune Inn, The Boiler Room, The Sting, Sports Palace, The Hanover House, The Space (Worcester)—and all the basements and VFW halls that I considered my real classrooms.

I have so many great memories from those days, simple things, like the excitement of finally finding that record or CD after searching for months through various distros. Or skateboarding outside of the club before the show. Trying to have philosophical discussions about veganism and straight edge, but really sounding like a complete idiot. Or jumping on stage during one of my favorite bands' sets and screaming into the mic that one line of a song that touched me a little deeper than the rest. Maybe I'm over-romanticizing all of this, maybe not.

What I realized, however, was that those were the first times I connected deeply with the things I was passionate about—skateboarding, punk rock, ideological exploration, and so forth—and what made those experiences so meaningful was the sincerity and emotions they produced, thus making them spiritual for me. Realizing that, I understood that spirituality has always been *the path*. For example, growing up, things like punk, movies, art, and skateboarding touched my heart, they were my spiritual teachings, and continue to be a large part of my spiritual growth to this very day.

So in the spirit of nostalgia and the community ethics that were once at the forefront of the punk/hardcore movement, I decided that instead of posing all of the questions for Ian myself, I'd ask some old-school punk/hardcore friends what they'd like to ask him as well. There were a number of awesome questions submitted, but one from Nate Newton (bassist for Converge) resulted in an answer from Ian that would later prove to have a significant impact on me. Nate's question was simply: "Do you still get on your skateboard and how has skateboarding influenced your life/impacted your relationship with punk?"[2]

The following is only a portion of Ian's insightful and extensive answer, as it's specifically what relates to my own subsequent experience that I'll explain in a moment.

My relationship with skateboarding in the seventies, when I first started, was a way to develop the ability to redefine the world around me, so skateboarding became a discipline and

everything in the world changed in terms of how it applies
to a skateboard. For instance, the other day I went outside
and somebody had dumped a bunch of water in the alley and
it had frozen, so I had the thought, **skateboarding**
even though I don't really ride much
anymore, but I automatically thought **became a**
of skateboarding and that's just how **discipline**
my brain works.

Weather has a different relationship if you're a skateboarder—sidewalks, swimming pools, curbs, banks. I was
walking in the Washington D.C. subway system and the
walls have a smooth curled transition and there's a railing
there and I thought about if I was to ride up that transition
what the compression would be to get to the vertical flat. So
in other words, I think that skateboarding taught me how to
look at the world in a different way and to relate things in
terms of how I was going to approach them.[3]

Skateboarding has been a passion of mine since the early 80s,
which makes it easy for me to relate to Ian's explanation of how it
can change one's worldview. While visiting New York City recently,
I thought about Ian's statement as I rode a very congested subway,
but instead of using skateboarding as a reference, I used spirituality.

Today, spirituality has definitely redefined my worldview. Just as
Ian and I see things like sidewalks, swimming pools, curbs, banks,
and so forth in relation to skateboarding, I also see similar everyday things—and people—in relation to spirituality. And, just as Ian
contemplated the curled transition and railing in the D.C. subway in
relation to skateboarding, I contemplated my interconnectedness to
all beings while traveling the subways of New York City.

There were, of course, the people who are easy to relate to:
the children smiling haphazardly about whatever simple wonders
caught their attention in the moment, or the younger punk and
hip-hop people (*real* hip-hop heads, not the radio pop music that is
passed off as hip-hop today . . . yeah, I said it). But there was also the

angry man in his fifties, wearing a suit and swearing under his breath at "the stupid son of a bitch" who accidentally bumped into him, and the men and women dressed to the nines, who were obviously headed to the club, and the homeless person half asleep and tucked away in the corner. What about them?

While on the subway, I caught myself judging people completely based on their outward appearance. I didn't think that I was better or worse than any of them, but I was reducing them to a label based on appearance. It didn't matter whether it was the people I felt I could relate to or not; I was still separating them, *all of them*, by seeing them as other than myself. I only saw the children as the children, the angry man as the angry man, the club people as the club people, and the homeless man as the homeless man. I'd completely forgotten everything I've been talking about in this book and was lost in my own sheltered world of separating thoughts. The beautiful thing, however, is that sooner, rather than later, I caught myself, which served as a wonderful reminder that, in fact, cultivating spirituality and practices truly does work, and very well at that.

Some of us may find that we judge ourselves for judging others (like I do at times), but it's so important to be compassionate toward ourselves if and when we make that connection. It's easy to mentally condemn ourselves for having those thoughts, especially since we're supposed to be spiritual people. The fact is, however, we're learning, practicing, and growing. We're working from where we are *now*, toward cultivating greater awareness of these areas in our lives, and that's what matters the most. Again, please be compassionate toward

Compassion toward others is crucial

yourself. We have a lot of conditioning that's been instilled in us since birth, and it takes time to undo. So be patient in the process and rest assured that it's working itself out.

Compassion toward others is equally as crucial, because we never truly know what another person is going through. That stranger sitting across from us, our co-workers, the cashier at our local store, all of whom may have a miserable demeanor—who knows what's going on in their life. Maybe they just lost their job, or were dumped, or received some very disheartening news about a family member. We never really know what internal struggles others are facing—so, by cultivating compassion for all beings, each one of us lessens the suffering of humanity as a whole (ourselves included). Each one of us truly can make a difference.

10

HOLY GRAIL SALE

*All over the place, from the popular culture
to the propaganda system,
there is constant pressure to make people
feel that they are helpless,
that the only role they can have is to
ratify decisions and to consume.*

Noam Chomsky

I recently read an article in *The New York Times* titled "The New Mantra: Replacing 'Om' with 'Glam.'" The headline read: "BEFORE MEDITATING AND LOOKING GOOD WITHIN, MAKE SURE TO LOOK GOOD ON THE OUTSIDE TOO."[4]

My stomach turned.

I knew it wasn't going to be an easy read, but my curiosity got the better of me, and I indulged. After finishing, I definitely felt twisted up inside. This is actually my second attempt at writing about it, because my first one was nothing more than a scathing rant, which does no one any good (save my own ego, of course).

The article essentially celebrates and glorifies fashionable spirituality in a way that would have even Chögyam Trungpa shaking his head in the heavenly realms of Shambala. The first paragraph of the article explains:

> For a new generation of "spiritual seekers," a daily meditation practice has become the emotional equivalent of green juice: a well-being essential. Russell Brand has described it

as "like a shower for your brain," while the Victoria's Secret model Miranda Kerr has said it helps her stay in goddess-like shape, inside and out. And when "transcendental" and "trendy" appear in the same sentence, one question inevitably comes to mind (no matter how hard you are trying to empty the contents of your cranium): What to wear?

Really, that's the *one question* that inevitably comes to mind? "What to wear?" And really, you're using Russell Brand and a Victoria's Secret model to validate the practice of meditation. I'm actually quite fond of Russell Brand, and I think it's great that he and Miranda Kerr both have a meditation practice, but if that's the example the *New York Times* chooses to show the world what spirituality and meditation look like, well, therein lies a big part of the problem. That's also not to say it has to look like monks in robes with shaved heads, but how about some middle ground? I mean, unless I missed the memo, spirituality is not just for pretty, clean-cut, white folks who have more money than they know what to do with, which is exactly the image this article is promoting through its choice of sources.

"The New Mantra" goes on to shamelessly promote ridiculously overpriced and completely unnecessary yoga and meditation products, such as Devotion Long-Sleeve Tee ($68), Intuition Sweater Wrap ($178), the Please Me Pullover ($118), and the coup de grâce, $995 sweat/yoga pants from Donna Karan's Urban Zen line. The only question I'm left asking myself is, what the fuck is going on here?!

Part of why this left me feeling queasy is that things are obviously changing energetically on our planet. More people than ever are beginning to wake up and explore spirituality, which is amazing. Many of these people, however, are in a very vulnerable place. Let's face it, many of us seek out spirituality because our lives aren't fulfilling in the first place, right? We need to find something with real substance to fill that void in our hearts, which things like sex, food, drugs, and shopping don't do on more than a very fleeting and temporary basis. And depending on just how hurt or impressionable a person is when coming into their own spirituality, some honestly may not have the capacity at the time to see through the vulture-esque nature of these companies that scavenge on vulnerable new seekers.

Another thing to consider is that these companies, as well as the people who buy their products, are overlooking the fact that *spirituality* is just a word, and *yoga* and *meditation*, they're just words too. The heart of any practice always comes from within, and never, *ever* from without. What's happening here with these pricey trends is the equivalent of people going to church on Sundays with the intention of *buying* their way into heaven when the collection basket is passed.

You *can't* buy a spiritual experience, nor will overpriced clothing bring your meditation practice to a place of enlightenment any quicker. Sure, I guess you might look fabulous in some people's eyes, but if that's the mind-set you're going into your practice with—dressing to impress—well, I honestly can't think of a nice way to finish this sentence, so I'll leave it up to you to fill in the blank.

I acknowledge that, on a personal level, the majority of this article is my ego writing about its disappointment in other people's egos, and how it's a huge disservice to spirituality. And I can sit here all day and talk to you about why business and spirituality can be a toxic combination when conducted in ways such as the aforementioned companies do, but when all is said and done, that's all it is, just talk.

You can't buy a spiritual experience

On a deeper level, however, a part of this comes from a place within me that doesn't speak in words. A place where, underneath my egoic frustration toward what "The New Mantra" has to say, is a very sincere sadness. I'm disheartened that much of what our culture is coming to accept, embrace, honor, and celebrate as spirituality is nothing more than a price tag on empty fashions, kitschy catch phrases, and gimmick after gimmick.

Many teachers and students forget that, at the end of the day, it's all about heart and reconnecting with our higher self, the self that can't be accessed through an article in the *New York Times* or even what I'm writing about here. The answers, *everything* we're searching for, they're already within us. They simply sit, waiting patiently to be remembered. And as we cultivate a sincere practice of meditation or yoga or any other method of reconnecting with our higher self, these answers, without fail, will reveal themselves to us.

And that, my friends, is something you can't put a price tag on.

11

WHEN THE BOTTOM GIVES OUT

Unless we agree to suffer we cannot be free from suffering.

D. T. Suzuki

Part of the insanity of addiction, at least in my experience, is that, in a very strange way, the more fucked up and chaotic the situations I found myself in, or the closer to death my actions brought me, the more alive I felt. Sadly, in retrospect, those experiences were the only times during that period of my life that I felt any semblance of life coursing through my veins.

Throughout my years of attending twelve-step meetings, I've often heard the disease of addiction referred to as cunning, baffling, and powerful, and as someone who's lived through it, I find even that is an understatement. I still experience the bafflement today, as I **cunning, baffling, and powerful** catch myself occasionally romanticizing the thoughts and memories of those very dark experiences when they arise. I know this is fucked up, but a part of me still feels a very strange sense of excitement and aliveness when I think about withdrawals spent hovering over a toilet bowl, or leaving the emergency room only to go immediately to the package store and pick up where I left off the night before (which has happened on more than one occasion).

Whenever I find myself romanticizing those thoughts, however, I do my best to use them as a reminder that today I no longer need to hide from my thoughts and emotions. I can mindfully see those insane thoughts for exactly what they are—which is simply, insane thoughts. I don't need to live in denial of having them, and today I'm grateful to recognize that they're just more grist for the spiritual mill.

 "Perils of the Living" by Chris Grosso.
http://www.beyondword.com/indiespiritualist/
audiodownload6.m4a

12

HEY, ASSHOLE

Imperfection is not our personal problem—
it is a natural part of existing.

Tara Brach

We're all assholes sometimes, myself very much included. I'm not proud of it, but if I'm truly dedicated to becoming a better person and cultivating greater compassion for myself and others, I need to be honest about this.

The thing is, though, people are typically the biggest assholes toward themselves. For example, I was a particularly big asshole to myself while finishing up the rough draft of this book for my editors. Thoughts like "You're a terrible writer" and "You don't have anything of worth to say" and "You're setting yourself up for embarrassment and failure" have made temporary residence in my mind. And for one reason or another, I've allowed them to stay . . . but why?

I mean, if I overheard someone saying any of that shit to someone else, whether it was a friend, family member, or even a complete stranger, I know I would step in on their behalf, and I'm guessing that most likely many of you would too. Yet, when it comes to the self-inflicted asshole syndrome, we usually just let it ride.

So why is it that so many of us feel unworthy of the very same love we so freely share with other people? And why is it easier to

45

show compassion to a complete stranger than to the person looking back at us in the mirror?

My very honest and simple answer is, I don't know. I mean, sure, I could offer you a handful of spiritual and psychological theories, things I've personally learned and implemented throughout my life, some of which have helped, and some of which I've found to be a complete waste of time. However, the fact remains that the self-negating thoughts still arise.

I used to try to play spiritual superhero by suppressing these thoughts. Or, when it was too difficult to suppress them, I'd lie to myself and pretend like they didn't bother me (which was obviously a complete crock of shit). But it's through facing these thoughts and acknowledging the mental and emotional impact they have on me, rather than pretending like they don't exist and that everything is double rainbows and unicorns, that they begin to happen less frequently and with less force behind them.

So I guess the one completely cliché spiritual thing I'll leave you with, which I find works significantly well in guiding the mind away from asshole territory, is to remind myself, again and again, that underneath our material forms, we really are all *One*.

And remember, when Ram Dass said, "Treat everyone you meet like God in drag," he didn't mean everyone except *yourself*. Because *you*, you're just God in drag too, silly. So stop being an asshole toward God, okay?

13

BUT I'M NOT INTERESTED IN YOGA, So Now What?!

*Once you take yourself too seriously,
the art will suffer.*

Maynard James Keenan

You see, it's not that I have any problem with yoga.

Actually, I have a lot of respect for it and for those who are sincere practitioners. I mean, my wonderful wife is a longtime yogini, as are many of my dear friends, but it's just never been my cup of tea. I tried Bikram and Kundalini and other forms of asana (yoga of posturing) some years ago, but it just isn't my thing.

What I notice these days, however, is that if you're involved in pretty much any kind of spiritual seeking and say that you don't do yoga, well, there's no shortage of folks who will look at you as some kind of spiritual blasphemer. To them I say, don't get your leggings in a bunch.

In the spirit of keeping things light, however, and admitting that my lack of knowledge may play somewhat of a role in this, allow me to share two recent stories that make clear just how out of touch with yoga I truly am. I share these in good fun and in the spirit of being able to laugh at ourselves.

I'm a kirtan musician (yup, I can already hear some of you saying, "Kirtan musician but not a yoga practitioner!?") and am honored to perform with the wonderfully gifted yoga instructor Alanna Kai-valya, who, luckily for me, also has a great sense of humor. We recently played at Yoga Journal's conference in Estes Park, Colorado, and the following is a loose translation of the conversation we had after Alanna picked me up at the Denver airport upon my arrival:

Me: So, this is cool. I've never been to Colorado. I can't wait to check out the mountains and elk.

Alanna: Yeah, it's beautiful. I grew up here and am sure you'll love it.

Me: Yeah, awesome. So Yoga Journal—is that a website or something?

Alanna: Are you fucking serious?

Me: Yeah, why?

Alanna: You're such a shit. Ten years ago I saved and scraped together every penny I had so I could attend my first conference, with the dream of one day teaching at it, which I'm now blessed to do. And here you waltz, VIP musician status, in to one of the country's biggest yoga events of the year, and you don't even know what it is!?

Me: Yeah, that sounds about right. Um, I'm sorry?

That was definitely a playful exchange, but, I mean, I didn't even know what *Yoga Journal* was. I must say that it was an amazing experience, however, and the folks who ran the event were exceptionally kind and generous people, so it really was a pleasure meeting and spending time with both them and the students who attended.

This second story comes from the studio where Alanna and I were recording some of said kirtan songs. This time, our dear friend and managing editor for *Elephant Journal*, Kate Bartolotta, was there to witness the ridiculousness.

As we finished recording a track called "Orange Sky," Alanna and Kate were talking about how it'd be a perfect song for *savasana*, or corpse pose. I interjected, asking them what a savasana was. (I actually just had to Google how to spell *savasana*. No, really, I did.) The look on both of their faces was priceless. Bewildered, Kate said something to the effect of, "You're recording a kirtan album and don't know what savasana is?"

The thing is, up until that point, I really didn't. The yoga I find myself attracted to comes from the other branches, which are significantly less popular than asana, including bhakti (yoga of devotion), jnana (path of knowledge), and karma yoga (discipline of action), because those are what resonate for me.

Of course, the body positions assumed in asana yoga are an important expression of joining with God. It's just that it's not the only way, and I wish some people were more accepting of that. Reminiscent of the outcast skateboarder in high school, I find myself feeling ostracized at times.

It gets old, being judged for not being a yoga practitioner in the asana sense. I mean, I love meditation, reading, running, and other various forms of exercise, and definitely am aware of my connection to the Collective Consciousness during much of them. I also believe I'm connecting with Spirit not only through those activities but anytime I bring my awareness to it—hell, even as I'm typing these words.

As I've come to understand and experience this whole spirituality thing, there's never a time I'm not connected to Spirit. Honestly, all bullshit aside, it doesn't matter if I'm some über yogi—or whatever else: a cave monk in Thailand,

all bullshit aside, it doesn't matter if I'm some über yogi

a priest in the Vatican, or the Dalai Lama himself. You and I are equally as connected to this Collective Consciousness, regardless of the way we choose to pursue it (or even not pursue it), because we already are It. *Tat tvam asi*, thou art that. It's not just a cool, cliché saying from the Upanishads, but a very sincere truth.

So with that being said, let's all support one another on our paths, regardless of the differences, okay? I promise not to make fun of *your* downward dog if you promise not to make fun of *my* lack of yoga gear and asana knowledge. Cool?

14

NEW NOISE

*After silence, that which comes nearest to
expressing the inexpressible is music.*

Aldous Huxley

I t's unfortunate that many spiritual circles can be very judgmental, especially regarding the types of music that practitioners listen to. I mean, my love of heavy music, metal, punk, and hardcore has earned me frowns on more than one occasion from *veteran* practitioners of various faiths. It's as if my practice or appreciation of spirituality is less significant than theirs because I don't fit the traditional mold, and that's really too bad. Instead of begrudging those who choose to judge, however, it's a wonderful reminder that I'm comfortable in my skin, my outer appearance, and the music I listen to, knowing that those things do not make me any less spiritual than anyone else, nor do they you.

Meditation, mantra, and prayers are valid when they are coming from a sincere heart, regardless of what our external appearance reflects or what music we choose to listen to. And besides, it's not like I roll into a meditation group's parking lot blasting *Master of Puppets*, though, sure, I'll rock a band shirt if it's what I happen to be wearing that day.

I shouldn't be totally shocked by the perplexed or even disapproving looks I get when I have band names such as Deadguy or High on Fire blaring across my chest when I walk into holy and sacred spaces. But really, why does anyone care? Why is it considered more spiritual to wear Ganesh T-shirts, suits and ties, sweaters, leggings, pretty dresses, and so forth? Did some of us miss the memo about proper worship attire?

I don't go out of my way to wear shirts that will catch people's attention, just as I don't go out of my way to change what I already have on for the day. Can you imagine walking into a room to meditate with Christ, Buddha, or Krishna, and them giving you the stink eye because of what you're wearing? Isn't the point of meditation groups or other *holy* institutions to quiet the mind, or to praise the Beloved (depending on what tradition you're practicing), not judge what others happen to be wearing on any given day?

This may sound insignificant to some, but I truly believe it's important to consider. Especially because it can leave people who are newly interested in spirituality, especially those who don't fit the traditional image of what practitioners are "supposed" to look like, completely turned off. Imagine stepping out of your comfort zone and attending church, or meditation group, or some other spiritual gathering for the first time, only to feel ostracized due to your appearance. Sucks, right?

Someone actually wrote to me once after reading an article I'd written about the influence that punk/hardcore music had on me at an early age in terms of learning how to honor my own truths. The woman told me that it was refreshing for her to read that, because she is judged by friends for liking hard rock music. She went on to say that, when her "spiritual" friends came over, they'd give her a very hard time for owning such CDs. So much so, in fact, that it got to the point where she would hide them before they came over, because she felt that was the easiest solution.

I understand her not wanting to deal with confronting her friends and, thus, hiding her CDs rather than making it an issue. Some of you might be thinking that she should have just dumped them as friends, moved on, and been done with them. And sure, that's definitely an option. However, this situation could also have been an excellent opportunity for her to grow in the confidence of exactly who she is on her spiritual path. Instead of hiding her CDs, or simply writing her friends off, she could have, in a very compassionate yet firm way, explained to them that what resonates with her on her own spiritual path doesn't need to be the same thing that resonates for them on theirs. Then, if her friends still aren't willing to accept her for who she is and what she likes, she would know she's done all that she can to try and rectify the situation, and then make whatever decision that feels right for her moving forward.

Many of us as independent-thinking spiritualists are faced with situations like these quite often, and as we become more deeply rooted in a place of acceptance and mindfulness, we're able to be compassionate rather than reactive toward others, even when they're not willing to do the same for us. And it's in our ability to do this, to offer compassion rather than reaction, that we reaffirm the fact that our spiritual practice is indeed on course. Back in the day, the old Chris, who had no interest in spirituality, would have simply told someone to fuck off if they rubbed him the wrong way. And while, sure, I may mentally still do that from time to time, it's less frequent these days.

15

LITTLE DID I KNOW

When the light turns green, you go.
When the light turns red, you stop.
But what do you do when the light turns blue with
orange and lavender spots?

Shel Silverstein, A Light in the Attic

My first time taking LSD is something I'll never forget. It was the night of my sixteenth birthday, a weeknight, which meant I had school the next morning. I was a senior, and one of my close friends and I had set up our schedules for the year so that we didn't have to be in until third period. So we made a plan for him to spend the night at my house so we could drop acid. We'd already been drinking vodka and smoking pot in the mornings on our way to school, so I figured, why not.

While today I am in recovery from active addiction and personally don't promote the use of drugs (though, to each their own), I do recognize and honor my first trip, and the countless subsequent trips I embarked on after that, as having a huge impact on the expansion of my consciousness. This may rattle some cages, but I do believe there can be positive (and, of course, negative) things that come with the use of *certain* drugs.

this may rattle some cages

I loved my LSD experience right from the start. I'll never forget the way it made my body feel—as though it were melting and yet warm, with all of my senses coming alive in a way that made pot seem like child's play. After roughly an hour from the time we'd taken the acid, I began to see visual effects, which were nothing short of brilliant. The swirling, pulsating nature of my sensory experience was, without my knowledge, the first glimpse of higher consciousness and ego unraveling that I would experience.

My friend and I stayed up all night, and, as the hours passed, the visuals continued to intensify. As the early morning hours crept their way into the experience (which seemed to go on for months rather than hours), some semblance of normalcy began to return to me, and at the same time a part of me knew I'd never be the same again. Eventually it was time for us to head to school, so we decided to drop a couple more tabs of acid before leaving. I was feeling good and had been in the experience long enough at that point that I felt confident in my abilities to navigate more of it through school. It was only moments after arriving in class, however, that an announcement came over the loudspeaker, stating that all juniors and seniors would be going to the auditorium for a viewing of Schindler's List. Somehow, I'd totally spaced on the fact that they were going to be showing it to us that day, and it was obviously not what I'd wanted to hear. Seeing as though I was not in an entirely sound state of mind, however, it never occurred to me to just bail and go somewhere else. Thus, the one and only time I've ever seen

I was an addict from the very start

Schindler's List was while I was engrossed in an epic acid trip, and it sucked.

I made it through the film and the day (though it wasn't easy), and seeing as how my friend and I had survived such an ordeal, we decided to celebrate by—drum roll, please—taking more acid. Later that night, a friend was actually throwing a co-birthday party for myself and another friend, and we continued tripping well into the early hours of the following morning. So my first acid experience lasted a solid day and a half, and I was in love.

While it may sound like I'm glorifying this experience, that's not my intention. Yes, it was fun (minus *Schindler's List*), but my goal here is to paint the picture for you that I was an addict from the very start. I mean, even as a kid I remember having very addictive eating habits, a behavior that obviously carried over to the way I used drugs in my later years.

Little did I know . . . little did I know.

16

QUESTION EVERYTHING

In a society that tries to standardize thinking,
individuality is not highly prized.

Alex Grey

When I say "question everything," I don't mean it in a conspiracy theorist sort of way (though even that has its place at times), but rather in a constructive way that suggests we check in with ourselves, quieting our mind and looking within our heart to feel whether we're honoring our deepest truths at any given moment. When we question everything, we go deeper into our own personal experience in order to find out what resonates with, and truly works for, us on our journey.

Creating a safe, nurturing, and supportive space for seekers from all paths and walks of life is of paramount importance, especially in this day and age when many feel spiritually out of place. I mean, doesn't it seem like our natural tendency should be to celebrate our differences, rather than completely discredit one another because of them?

Why are some people so scared of others' beliefs, particularly regarding religion and spirituality, that they completely discredit what they have to say simply because it doesn't coincide with their own views or experiences?

There's no shortage of things that baffle me in life, but exclusion based on different beliefs is one that definitely tops the list. A lot of people automatically think of Christianity and Catholicism when they think of closed-minded religious and spiritual sects, but it's rampant in all religions and spiritualties, including, but not limited to, Judaism, Buddhism, Hinduism, and so forth.

We all have our core beliefs, and many of them have served us well. We've had many wonderful things instilled in us since birth, plenty of which are still very useful today. Many of us, however (myself included), have also picked up plenty of things that have seeped into our unconscious and definitely don't serve our, or anyone else's, best interests. The good news, however, is that it's much easier to change these outdated paradigms than you may think.

Simply exploring why something doesn't resonate with us—and bringing mindful attention to our conditioned belief systems—puts us well on our way. This is also a good time for me to mention meditation, as it's a wonderful complementary practice. Through meditation, our minds begin to quiet, which, in turn, allows new realizations and fresh ideas to make their way to our consciousness. It may not necessarily happen while we're formally sitting in meditation itself. But when we give our mind some quietude, the results carry over into our everyday lives, making it easier for insights and clarity to present themselves at any given moment throughout the day.

As we go about our days, spending more time in mindfulness and inquiry, we'll become clearer on the most current truths that resonate and serve us, and we'll become more deeply rooted in them. We'll establish a deeper sense of trust in our own intuition, which will guide us unfailingly if we allow it.

Our own well-being is up to us and no one else. By making the conscious effort to bring awareness and inquiry to our emotional states during the times we'd normally blame someone or something else, we are regaining control. We are questioning, we are learning, and we are taking back our power.

17

HEROES?

Most of my heroes don't appear on no stamps.
Public Enemy, "Fight The Power"

What is a role model, a hero? Traditionally speaking, sure, it's a person we look to as an example of someone we aspire to be like based on their courage and other noble qualities. But as I look around today at those who are celebrated as role models by popular media, I find myself left with little more to say than: What. The. Fuck.

It's as if the majority of today's role models and heroes are part of a machine that's sole purpose is cutting costs by manufacturing more of the same. With that being the predominant source of inspiration for much of today's youth, well, finding one's own voice, thoughts, and personality is not easily accomplished. And if you're one of the few who sets out on their own path, not caring about conforming to popular trends, chances are better than not that you're in for some rough years ahead.

With that being said, it may seem like an easier option to just go ahead and get on with conforming now, because, really, isn't life hard enough already without the added element of breaking norms? The short-term answer would be yes, of course. Life would probably be much simpler if we were to just do what society wants us to do. Listen to the music the radio tells us to listen to, watch the movies the coolest actors are in, read the books that everyone else is reading, and so forth, but I promise you this, in the long run, if your heart is trying to guide you to places other than the traditional norms, it will eventually catch up with you and begin to weigh heavily.

That's why I'm grateful that I grew up feeling a connection to unconventional role models and heroes such as professional skateboarder Mike Vallely. I found that I always appreciated Mike for his zero-bullshit approach to, well, basically everything. I first became aware of Mike in the late 80s when I saw him in Powell-Peralta's *Public Domain* skateboarding video. Later, I came to see Mike almost as a physical manifestation of the punk rock/hardcore music I'd come to draw so much inspiration from.

Throughout my youth, and still to this day, I've read and watched interviews with Mike. He often tells people, with strong conviction, to be themselves and do their own thing regardless of what others think. I remember that being something I specifically drew a lot of inspiration from early on in my spiritual journey.

As I first set out on my spiritual exploration, it wasn't like there was a cool, or even an uncool, group of people that I was trying to emulate. No, that definitely wasn't the case, because, in actuality, no one I knew gave two shits about anything even remotely related to spirituality. So it was during the initial stages of my spiritual endeavor—the times I felt even more alone than usual, since there was no one around to discuss spirituality with—that I remembered the inspiration I'd received from Mike's words, as well as from my punk roots, which consistently inspired me to honor *my* truth and be myself regardless of what others thought. It's like what Q-Tip from A Tribe Called Quest says in "Steve Biko (Stir It Up)": "I am recognizing that the voice inside my head is urging me to be myself but never follow someone else." I sincerely did (and still do) my best to live those words.

I honored what was in my heart, which was the undeniable call for something more, something deeper than what I'd found up to that point in my life. I think that call is something we all share in common—our hearts call for something more. However, for whatever reason, some of us just happen to find ourselves in situations where we're able to hear it a little more clearly and feel it a little more deeply.

Whether we decide to get on with it today, next month, or ten years from now, the call will wait. The question I invite you to ask yourself is, "Do you really want to keep pretending like you don't hear it, like you don't feel it?"

If you decide that you don't want to ignore it any longer, and it's in fact time to begin your journey down the proverbial rabbit hole, it's important to know that the paths other individuals take often look and sound much different than the one you may find yourself on. And that's the beauty behind the concept of Indie Spirituality: it's all relevant, and it's all to be honored. Our own personal experiences are perfect for our spiritual growth, even if there's nothing traditionally spiritual about them.

I mean, like I said, I still draw inspiration from Mike V. to this day, regardless of whether he has any interest in spirituality. His words and lifestyle inspire me to carry on with what resonates as truth in my heart, spiritual or otherwise. In an interview I did with Mike for The Indie Spiritualist website, he shared some simple yet profound insight about much of what I've been talking about here:

> Role models and heroes are vital, and I think a big problem in our society is that we don't have heroes anymore, or maybe the heroes we have are just so full of shit it trickles down, but those aren't heroes, it's something else. I grew up with heroes, people who made me aspire to raise my game, to dream bigger and I like to keep it that simple. Everything that I'm really about is being an individualist. I believe in individuality. I'm not out here on the front lines trying to create clones, or consumers, or worshippers of who I am, and what I do. I'm trying to nurture the idea that you should do your own thing, which is really powerful. I don't like to get too involved in the idea that "I'm a role model" and that

everything I do is right. I don't think that's the case at all, but I think who I am at my core, and what I represent at my core, is something that is meaningful, and can be something that other people can gain inspiration from. That's not necessarily what drives me, but that's also what I think makes it that much more powerful.[5]

Fucking *amen*, Mike! It was so validating to hear him talk about nurturing the idea that we should do our own thing, and

Fucking amen

his emphasis on cultivating individuality. He inadvertently described exactly what the Indie Spiritualist model is all about—which is being unapologetically yourself. Honoring your truth and celebrating who you are regardless of what anyone else thinks. What a boring world we'd live in if, like Mike said, we were all just clones.

18

TRANSCENDENCE

I fell asleep in a world dressed in grey
Only to awake in a garden divine

Isis, "Garden of Light"

I was fortunate to interview Aaron Turner, frontman for the iconic band Isis, shortly after their breakup in 2010. I'd heard that Aaron had an interest in spirituality, and I was very curious as to what spirituality looked like for him, as he and Isis were monumental in the post-metal, ambient/drone music movement. And as we've already established, the two aren't typically associated with one another. In response, Aaron said:

> I guess the closest thing I could say about my idea of spirituality and how that plays into Isis is that Isis is an outlet of expression for me. It's a way to explore things inside myself and make sense of those things as they relate to the world around me. It was also a way for me to tap into an energy, and state of consciousness, which was not accessible to me in most other areas of my life. It allowed me, at times anyway, to reach a sort of level of transcendence, and I feel that's a very spiritual thing.[6]

A state of transcendence, like the same state of transcendence that happens in a traditionally spiritual music setting such as kirtan? Yup, absolutely, and I speak from personal experience in regard to both. I've been to that transcendent place while chanting to God along with

two sides
of the
same coin

Krishna Das, just as I have been while listening to Isis's pulsating riffs. They are two sides of the same coin. Knowing that many spiritual types wouldn't buy that, however, I asked Aaron to elaborate on the relationship between Isis's music and meditative states, to which he replied:

> Well I think there are certain aspects of our music that are very meditative. Some of what I found interesting about doing Isis was the sort of meditative and ritualistic aspects of it. I think there is something about this type of music that maybe lends itself to personal and spiritual experiences. The songs are long and very often have some underlying droney element, which allows the listener's consciousness to stretch out rather than just being completely bombarded through-out the song or album, especially with the earlier material, which was really repetitive.
>
> There was an element that I thought, rather than being monotonous, was sort of hypnotic. These are things which share some common ground with certain religious prac-tices, like the idea of a repetitive cyclic mantra and certain religious music which is sort of based in a drone oriented approach. Also, through the repetition of certain actions, or in this case musical actions, it's like you're summon-ing something, or creating an openness that allows your mind to let go of your very conscious, rational forebrain and peek into something deeper and wider. Hopefully, in some way or another, this will connect you with the world around you, and perhaps other people who are sharing in that experience.[7]

I find both of Aaron's answers to be nothing short of profound, but I'd like to emphasize one line particularly for your consideration: "creating an openness that allows your mind to let go of your very conscious, rational forebrain and peek into something deeper and wider." And again: *creating an openness that allows your mind to let go of your very conscious, rational forebrain and peek into something deeper and wider.*

Isn't that the thesis of true, deep, spiritual aspiration, to cultivate and reach that place? So with that being said, I hope it's now clear that all music—heavy, soft, and everything in between—can be wonderful catalysts for spiritual experiences.

19

THE TAO OF CHECKING YOURSELF

Let it be still, and it will gradually become clear.

Lao Tzu, Tao Te Ching

I've been interviewing folks, well, as far back as my first zine, Speak Only When Spoken To, which I did back in high school. It was a shit zine, both in production and prose, but after writing some scathing pieces about the school's administration, it did force them to write a new rule in the school's handbook, saying something like distribution of non-approved material on school grounds is subject to suspension or expulsion.

Anyway, my first guest-list experience, resulting from an interview I did with Brad Wilk of Rage Against the Machine for *Speak Only When Spoken To*, was at New York City's Roseland Ballroom in '95 when he put me on the list for their show with The Jesus Lizard. So besides capitalizing on the opportunity to name-drop Brad Wilk, Rage Against the Machine, and The Jesus Lizard (hey, I'll call myself out as quickly as anyone else), my point here is that, since '95, I've never once had an issue with tickets, guest lists, or press credentials (which are typically set up by the band's management ahead of the show).

That is, until I recently found myself standing at the box office of the MGM Grand, on the phone with Naughty by Nature's tour manager, who informed me that the venue had completely dropped the ball and had no tickets or press credentials for any of the performers on the tour that night. He was still working on it, but couldn't promise anything, and said he'd get back to me shortly. Needless to say, the night was not off to a good start.

As I stood there, my initial reaction was definitely serious disappointment. My brother and I (he was supposed to be credentialed as well) were beyond excited not only to interview a hip-hop legend such as Treach, but also to see the show, as it featured some of our favorite hip-hop acts, including EPMD, Slick Rick, Rakim, Biz Markie, Big Daddy Kane, and more. What made matters even worse was that the show was sold out, so even if we wanted to we couldn't have bought tickets (not that my wallet minded keeping that seventy-five dollars, thank you very much).

So there we were, about an hour later and still no word, so I decided to call the tour manager back. He politely informed me that Treach was running a little late; instead of the 7:30 PM time that had been scheduled a few days earlier, the interview might have to wait until later on in the night, after their set finished and Treach had a chance to cool down. It wasn't definite, but it's how things were beginning to look.

At this point, I found myself feeling really frustrated. But the thing was, it wasn't directed at anyone or anything specific. It was just a cumulative frustration from the entire night seemingly going to shit. It would be fair to say that things like the Tao and mindfulness were the farthest thing from my experience in that moment. Not only that, but having never run into a problem like this before, I started feeling pretty entitled. I said to my brother, "Fuck it, I'm not feeling any of this. Let's just go." To which he luckily replied, "Well, do you want to wait to hear what the tour manager says about the interview first?" I said, "I guess. I don't know. I'm just really not feeling this." So with neither of us knowing what to do, we just stood there for a few minutes.

It was in those few minutes that I caught myself acting like an asshole about the situation. It wasn't that I was outwardly an asshole to anyone, but mentally I was acting like an entitled prick. I realized, Christ, I have an opportunity here to interview a fucking hip-hop legend, someone I've been a fan of since the early '90s, and I was willing to throw that away because everything wasn't going exactly as I'd expected it!?

The Tao. It's a force believed by many to underlie the creation of absolutely *everything* in existence, from the farthest reaches of the universe to the very hands we use to press play on our iPods.

The *Tao Te Ching* by Lao Tzu is Taoism's predominant piece of literature, and it provides readers with insight and teachings that are more philosophical and individualistic in nature than they are religious or dogmatic. The Tao talks about the flow of nature, the yin and yang (or female and male) energies of life, and, on an individual level, it emphasizes living a lifestyle that is in tune with nature and its surroundings, essentially teaching us to go with the flow of life and be open to spontaneity.

If it wasn't for learning to use the principles of the Tao, I would have missed out on the craziest concert experience of my life, even though it didn't start out like some mystical law-of-attraction type of thing, that's for sure. Nor was I all Zen'd out or in the flow when I found myself and my brother standing there twiddling our thumbs.

go with the flow of life

Putting all of that into perspective, I was suddenly able to smile at the ridiculousness of how I was thinking about this situation, and I resigned myself to just let it go and play out however it would. I mean, where was my spontaneity? Where was my flow in the Tao? It obviously wasn't there in that moment, but luckily I caught myself, and I was mentally back on track.

About five minutes later, the tour manager called me to ask where I was, which just so happened to be about ten feet away from where he was calling from. He said he was able to keep the interview time as scheduled, and he apologized for the venue not providing them with any tickets or passes, and for the overall inconvenience of the situation. I told him I knew it wasn't his fault and appreciated his help with the interview. Two minutes later, I was at Naughty by Nature's dressing room. The smell of what Snoop Dogg would call "the sticky icky" (aka really good weed), mixed with various types of liquor and beer, permeated the air as my brother and I were introduced to Treach.

We rocked out a quick ten-minute interview in the stairwell, since the dressing room was too noisy for my recording equipment. Treach was awesome. He gave candid answers to some tough questions, he was friendly, and most importantly he was real; he was authentic. After the interview, he told us he hoped we'd enjoy the show. When I told him that unfortunately we wouldn't be attending, as the venue fell through on tickets, his response was, "Nah, nah, y'all are gonna see the show. Come with me."

He brought us to the dressing room and told the tour manager we needed tickets, and the tour manager told Treach the same thing he'd told my brother and I, which was that there literally were none. At that point, Treach said, "Well, then they're coming down with us," and the manager gladly agreed.

We hung out for roughly ten minutes at the dressing room until it was time for Naughty by Nature to make their way to the stage. About ten of us piled into a big elevator, which took us directly to the back of the stage. As the doors opened, Vin Rock (Naughty by Nature's third member) greeted us and we all proceeded to the far side of the stage area. The walk was very dimly lit, and the only thing separating us from the crowd were some very tall black curtains.

The plan was to just hang out and watch Naughty's set from the side of the stage, which was beyond okay with us. As we stood there—my brother, Treach, Kay Gee, Vin Rock, and I, plus roughly ten other people from their entourage—waiting for Naughty by Nature to take the stage, a security guard approached us and said that everyone without passes would have to leave, which essentially was everyone except the band members, because, don't forget, the venue wouldn't issue any passes or tickets for the performers' friends or even media that night.

Treach told the security guard that we were all fine being there, because we were with him. The security guard said it wasn't fine, because we didn't have passes. They went back and forth for another minute before Treach finally said, "They're cool. They're coming on stage with me. They're part of the show." To which the security replied, "Who, these guys?" pointing to four big guys standing next to Treach. "No, all of them are coming on stage with me," Treach said, pointing to the entire group of us.

The security guard was obviously pissed, but what could he do? He stormed off, and Treach told us all to follow him up onto the stage and just plant ourselves on the riser so that the security guard(s) couldn't mess with us. I looked at my brother and asked him, "Um, is this really happening right now?" He didn't know how to respond. Everything had just been so surreal, starting with the moment we went up to their dressing room with the tour manager, and was only continuing to get crazier by the minute.

A few moments later a stagehand gave Treach and Vin Rock microphones. We were still out of sight from the audience when Treach and Vin began hyping them up by saying things like, "What's up, Connecticut?" and "Who's ready to party?" into their mics. Treach, lowering his mic for a second, looked at us and said, "Here we go, y'all." And sure enough, there we went. We followed him up the stairs to the riser where he'd told us to stand, and there we stood, next to their dee-jay, Kay Gee, for the entire set. Well, not the entire set exactly. During their last song, which is the hip-hop anthem of anthems, "Hip Hop Hooray," they motioned for us to come down from the riser and onto the main area of the stage, so we could join them in taking part in the infamous side-to-side hand waving that's an integral part of the song.

As the song ended, we followed Treach and Vin Rock back up the stairs to exit the stage. I was the last one in line, and as I got to the top of the stairs, before exiting, I stopped for a moment. I turned around and mindfully looked out at the sold-out audience and thought about the Tao, and about going with the flow of life, and how, if I had acted on my earlier frustrated impulse and just left, I would have missed this entire amazing experience.

I smiled in gratitude and then walked off the stage, where there were two security guards waiting for those of us without passes to be escorted out. Treach, sweaty and shirtless, gave my brother and me a hug, and I did my best to muster up a few words to express my gratitude to him for such an amazing experience.

We may not have been able to stay and see the rest of the show, but when all was said and done, that meant very little to me after the experience I'd just had, going with the flow.

 Besides having the craziest chain of events happen—from the interview with Treach almost falling through at the sold-out MGM Grand, to ending up in his dressing room and then literally on stage for Naughty by Nature's entire set . . . well, I also got an endorsement for the book! http://www.youtube.com/watch?v=QUI4-DeV85A

20

THE MEANING OF LIFE

Each of us is full of shit in our own special way.
We are all shitty little snowflakes
dancing in the universe.

Lewis Black

So "What is the meaning of life?" is sort of the ultimate question, right? No one can give you a definitive answer. I mean, if you were to ask a hundred different people, you'd probably get a hundred different answers, but that's a part of the beauty of life, that we're all able to experience it in our own special ways.

As for my two cents, I think I stumbled onto what life means for me awhile back—while perusing Facebook, of all things. I was scrolling down my news feed (procrastinating from something or other, I'm sure), when all of the sudden my eyes beheld one of the most illumined memes ever. It was a picture of Moses holding the Ten Commandments tablet. But instead of ten commandments, there were only two, which read, "Be cool" and "Don't be an asshole." And I must say, whoever created that silly little meme was definitely on to something.

Like it or not, we are all assholes sometimes, but if we understand that we all come from the same shared Divinity, our asshole tendencies will lessen exponentially. We will then be able to

Don't be an asshole

75

celebrate one another's joys, passions, and happiness with a sense of freedom and acceptance of who we, and they, are as human beings.

We no longer have to narrowly identify ourselves or others based on material things like the way we dress, the music we listen to, the way we pray or meditate, or the movies we watch. Many of our outdated and conditioned paradigms (whether they be spiritual, social, or otherwise) have been ingrained in us without our even knowing, but now that we are becoming aware of them, we're free to leave them, and the asshole tendencies they create, behind.

21

ME, MYSELF & I

Forgetting oneself is opening oneself.

Dōgen

I have no shortage of thoughts centered on *me* and how *everything,* everything, relates to and revolves around me. "I can't wait for the new Deftones album to come out." "I'm glad I picked up this Sharon Salzberg book." "I don't want to meditate today." "Are they *really* remaking *Evil Dead*?!" (Which I've subsequently seen and it was brutally excellent.) That is just a tiny fraction of the thoughts I've had in the past five minutes, all of which revolve around *me*, and while they're seemingly innocent enough, those were the *nice* ones.

There's also the condemning thoughts that rear their ugly heads. "I'm fat." "I'm a terrible writer." "I'm an awful musician." However, all of these thoughts—from the seemingly innocent to the obviously painful—all arise from the same place of ego conditioning. The moment I begin to take any of them too seriously, I give up the peace of my natural state of being and allow my thoughts—that is to say, the mindless wandering notions I buy in to when I'm not consciously watching them—to dictate my mental, emotional, and spiritual well-being.

The following is an excerpt from one of the most influential books I've read in my life, which is a real eye-opener in regard to

reconciling ego nature (and its subsequent thoughts) with cultivating
a sincere and authentic spiritual path. The book is Chögyam Trungpa
Rinpoche's *Cutting through Spiritual Materialism*, and, actually, you
may want to proceed to your nearest bookstore or online retailer and
buy yourself a copy as soon as you can. In the meantime, I offer you
this little snippet, as I find myself often revisiting it in the humble
attempt to keep myself in check while trying to live spiritually:

> We have come here to learn about spirituality. I trust the
> genuine quality of this search but we must question its
> nature. The problem is that ego can convert anything to
> its own use, even spirituality. Ego is constantly attempt-
> ing to acquire and apply the teachings of spirituality for its
> own benefit. The teachings are treated as an external thing,
> external to "me," a philosophy which we try to imitate. We
> do not actually want to identify with or become the teach-
> ings. So if our teacher speaks of renunciation of ego, we
> attempt to mimic renunciation of ego. We go through the
> motions, make the appropriate gestures, but we really do
> not want to sacrifice any part of our way of life. We become
> skillful actors, and while playing deaf and dumb to the real
> meaning of the teachings, we find some comfort in pre-
> tending to follow the path.[8]

Oof, I know that's a tough one to swallow. Trust me, I can't tell
you how many times I've caught myself doing exactly what Trungpa
talks about in that excerpt. I've come to realize that, yes, we all have
an ego, and it is what it is, but the more we bring our awareness to
it and how it plays out in our daily lives, the less we will buy in to it,
and our ego nature will begin to subside naturally.

"A Little Less Like Dying" by Chris Grosso.
http://www.beyondword.com/indiespiritualist/
audiodownload7.m4a

22

TO LET SLEEPING DOGS LIE

Wrong is wrong, no matter who says it.

Malcolm X

It was around 10:00 AM on a beautiful Friday morning in April. My fiancée and I stood at the end of my street, taking in the unseasonably warm sunshine as we waited for our friend, who was on her way to pick us up and bring us to the venue where we'd be getting married the following day.

She was running late, but it didn't matter, because we were perfectly happy just taking in the morning together. A police car came driving up the street and slowly came to a stop. Rolling down his window, the officer—in that condescending cop tone that isn't just for television and movies—asked my fiancée and me why we were standing there.

By the time he finished his question, I watched my emotions do a complete one-eighty, from a place of joy and excitement regarding the following day's nuptials, to one of tense, annoyed frustration that brought me right back to some old high-school N.W.A. "Fuck tha Police" mind-set.

You see, my fiancée and I were on public property and in a rural area at 10:00 AM, minding our own business, so it was beyond obvious that he only stopped because we're both covered in tattoos. I could have maybe tried to lie to myself about that if he'd made even the slightest effort to not come off in such a condescending way, but no such luck.

Still, even though I knew exactly what he was doing and was frustrated by it, I kept cool and played along. I calmly explained that we were waiting for my friend to come pick us up, even pointing to my house, which was less than a hundred feet from where we were standing, letting him know that I lived right there. Still, it became obvious that he had nothing better to do with himself that morning, so that wasn't good enough for him.

It bothered me to no end that I had to give him even that little information, because I knew we were being harassed strictly because of our appearance. Now, it'd be irresponsible of me to say that all cops are bad, because I know there are plenty who are good, honest, and hardworking individuals, who do their jobs well, without abusing power and authority. But this officer was definitely not one of them.

So like I said, even after politely telling him why my fiancée and I were standing there, and showing him exactly where I lived, it still wasn't good enough for him. He proceeded to ask me what my last name was, and it was at this point that my politeness began to subside. I did keep my calm and composure, but became aware of my heartbeat rising, the muscles in my body tightening, and the tone of my voice losing its pleasantness. I asked the officer why he needed to know my last name, to which he simply asked again, "What's your last name?" This exchange went back and forth a couple of times, with each becoming sterner on both sides, until finally I stopped for a moment and mentally weighed my options.

I thought about the fact that I was getting married the next day, and really had to consider how far I was willing to go with this cop. I can tell you with complete certainty that, had I not been getting married the next day, that cop would have had to take me to jail before he got my last name out of me. Not wanting to tell him my last name may seem petty to those readers who've had little to no interaction

with the police, but for those of us who have, and have experienced
firsthand the authority complexes many of them have, well, enough
just sometimes becomes enough.

That being said, I did begrudgingly tell him my last name, which,
for a second time, should have ended our interaction right there. But
nope, without hesitation, he immediately looked at my fiancée, who
was dumbfounded by the ridiculousness of the situation, and asked
her for her last name too. Begrudgingly, she told him. Getting what
he wanted, the officer then told us that he was just trying to get to
know people in the area (which was a complete crock of shit) and
drove away.

Obviously that experience really pissed me off, and it stayed with
me for the rest of the morning and into the early afternoon. I allowed
it to eat at me during what should have been a joyous time while my
fiancée and I were at the venue where we'd be getting married in less
than twenty-four hours.

So the moral of the story, besides the fact that some cops can be
complete assholes, is that there are still things that I allow to affect
me, that cause me to fall extremely short of sharing love, which is,
you know, only one of the main running themes in this book and all.

In retrospect, I now see the futility in the whole thing. I really
didn't need to feed into any of it. I could have just accepted the
fact that this cop was being a dick and
harassing my fiancée and me for dickish **we're**
reasons. I could have acknowledged that **bound to**
it was his own shit that was being played
out, but instead I fed into it and sank to **fall short**
his level, allowing his shit to become our
shit. Even while doing our best to live spiritual lives, we're bound to
fall short, all of us, even the teachers who try to fool their followers
into believing otherwise.

What I can say is that I know my practice must be working, since
I didn't end up handcuffed or in jail, so there's that.

23

JESUS, HITLER, BIEBER, Slayer & God

The eye with which I see God
is the eye with which he sees me.
My eye and the eye of God are one eye,
one vision, one knowledge, and one love.

Meister Eckhart

Now, to say I love Hitler as much as I love Jesus, or Justin Bieber as much as Slayer, is not an easy thing to do. The moment I say otherwise, however, I'm coming from a place of duality and separation. Trust me, I still spend plenty of time in that place, though gratefully it's much less frequent these days. When I lay aside my ego conditioning, however, I'm able to come to a place of awareness that recognizes the shared Divinity in Hitler and Justin Bieber, as much as in Jesus and Slayer. During these moments, I am connected to unity and thus more in line with God's mind rather than my own. What people tend to overlook or consciously ignore is that, if God is pure love, and nothing but, then God doesn't know what hate, separation, and judgment are, because pure love is just that—pure. How can love be pure if stipulations are attached?

Jesus and Slayer

One of the most well-known scriptures in Buddhism is the heart sutra. Within the heart sutra, there is a mantra that is said to calm all suffering and bring duality to a place of nonduality. The mantra is: *Gate gate pāragate pārasamgate bodhi svāhā* (translated as "Gone, gone, gone beyond, gone completely beyond").[9] Beyond the sense of you, me, ours, and theirs, there lies one infinite truth, and that truth, as countless people have experienced—from mystics and sages, to the parent who loses all sense of self when they look into the eyes of their child—is pure love, which at its core is where everything truly is One.

Advaita Vedanta is a non-dualistic Hindu philosophy based on the doctrine of the Upanishads, which can also help exponentially in our understanding of oneness. Advaita means "not two" (non-dual), and Vedanta means "the end of knowledge," and together they assert that non-duality is the path to knowledge, that absolute reality

non-duality is the path to knowledge

is beyond our personal perception and cognition, or our ego, which is the lens through which the majority of us spend most of our time looking. However, during times of pure present-moment awareness, times where the ego lens is not blurring our perception, we unite with the pure "I," or "Brahman" (in Vedic tradition), which is absolute awareness and stands alone. This unification allows us to experience *reality* in its truest form, a form which has no room for duality, judgments, separation, and so forth. It's a place where Justin Bieber is, in fact, just as awesome as Slayer because there is quite literally no difference between them.

This "I" is unconditional love and knows nothing but love. It is the love that is the deepest reality of who we all are, including you, me, Hitler, Christ, Bieber, and Slayer.

The material body and ego that was Hitler was a monster and I would never try to say otherwise. The amount of suffering, horror, and death he was responsible for is incomprehensible. However, the part of me that says he was a monster is my dualistic ego nature, the same dualistic ego nature that says Jesus was an illumined teacher of love and liberation. Those are both personal judgments and opinions based on my dualistic thought system.

If I was coming from a place of pure non-duality, however, the only thing in my awareness would be that of an all-inclusive love—a love that wouldn't even recognize Hitler or Jesus as separate beings because, in that place, they aren't. Their material bodies have been laid aside and their true nature is united in the One ultimate Source, whether you care to call it Spirit, Collective Conscious, Tao, Buddha Nature, Brahman, God, Goddess, or whatever else works for you.

24

WHEN FOREVER COMES CRASHING

Before we can become who we really are,
we must become conscious of the fact
that the person who we think we are, here and now,
is at best an impostor and a stranger.

Thomas Merton

While I recall plenty of minor awakening experiences throughout my life—little moments of pure mindfulness accompanied by a complete sense of serenity for no rhyme or reason—my first truly comprehensive awakening experience began at the age of twenty-five, while I was sitting on a couch in my loft apartment in Middletown, Connecticut.

At the time, I was enrolled in a program to become a drug and alcohol counselor, and had become close with my professor/student advisor. She was an earthy, political, and spiritual woman. I wasn't into spirituality myself at the time (though the following is what inspired me to begin visiting various sanghas and so forth as I mentioned in the introduction), but she had such an honest way about her, a way that always made me feel like I was at home while I was in her presence, that my mind naturally opened to what she would talk about. I would meet with her periodically in her office for the typical course check-ins, and my attention was always drawn to her desk and walls, as they were scattered with eclectic images and statues. The ones that would primarily catch my attention were those of Buddha and Mother Mary. I found it interesting that someone would have two different iconic spiritual figures together. From what I knew about spirituality up to that point, you picked one and went with it.

One spring afternoon, we had our check-in on a bench outside, as it was one of those perfect days that just had to be taken advantage of. At the time, my then-girlfriend and I were in the process of breaking up, and, as my professor and I sat there discussing next semester and the courses I would be taking, I was trying to hide my pain.

I failed miserably, however, and my professor broached my obvious melancholy and asked me what was going on. I gave her a vague answer, saying it was "girl trouble," trying to brush it off as no big deal, but she saw right through it. She proceeded to ask me if I was a reader. At the time I really wasn't (boy, how the times have changed), so I told her not really, but she still asked if I'd be willing to read a book if she were to loan it to me. While I really didn't want to—again, not being much of a reader at the time—I had developed a trust with her in an almost motherly sort of way, so I begrudgingly agreed.

Two days later, during class, she handed me a book called *The Power of Now* by Eckhart Tolle. These days, Eckhart Tolle is a household name, but this experience all went down well before he was on *The Oprah Winfrey Show* and selling millions of books, so I had no idea who he was or what the book was about. In retrospect, that really played in my favor, because I was still in a place mentally where, had

my life would never be the same

he been all over Oprah's show at the time, I never would have given him, or the book, the time of day. I was still very much enmeshed in my punk rock, "fuck the mainstream" mind-set (and okay, to a certain extent, I still am today).

When I returned home that evening after class, I sat on my uncomfortable couch, opened up the book, and by the time I finished reading the introduction and first few chapters, I knew my life would never be the same. The first time I read *The Power of Now*, I actually read it three times, cover to cover, in quick succession. I remember the liberating feeling the book's teachings produced in me. At times, I actually felt higher than any drug had ever made me feel, so, being the good addict that I was, I couldn't get enough. For the first time in my entire life, I understood what the phrase "having the rug pulled out from under you" meant. I spent more and more time on my annoyingly uncomfortable couch, which I otherwise normally avoided, completely enthralled by what Tolle had written.

An aspect that really stuck out to me while reading *The Power of Now* was Tolle's universal teaching style, and the fact that he incorporated Jesus, Buddha, Lao Tzu, and others into his message. It was the second time that someone with an eclectic interest in spirituality (the first being my professor) had had a significant impact on my life, and I recognized that I needed to honor that realization. The idea that I could grow spiritually from more than strictly one source, or path, resonated deeply with me, as I've never been one to agree with the "my way or the highway" mentality that seems to be prevalent in many religious teachings.

After I finished my third read-through of *The Power of Now*, I was completely hooked on spirituality and needed more. I began collecting books and teachings like a vinyl collector at a record fair. I remember making the local library my second home for quite a while (I actually think I still owe some late fees to the Russell Library in Middletown, Connecticut—sorry about that). I read everything I could get my hands on, from Thich Nhat Hanh to Paramahansa Yogananda, Ken Wilber to Krishnamurti, but the next spiritual teacher I found myself connecting with in a way that was almost beyond words, was Ram Dass.

Reading his book *Be Here Now* was my second literary spiritual awakening. From its cookbook-style teachings to its '70s counterculture language, I was in love. There was even a time, inspired by Ram Dass's crazy psilocybin stories, that I ate an eighth of mushrooms by myself on a Sunday afternoon in an attempt to "experience God."

It was the one and only time I'd ever ingested hallucinogens with a spiritual intention, and it subsequently became the one and only time I ever experienced a bad trip (minus the *Schindler's List* mishap, but that was only a portion of the trip). About two hours after taking the mushrooms, I ended up freaking out, as I'd never tripped alone before, and I felt like I was going to die. So in one of my most non-brilliant moments ever, I called my parents and asked them to come pick me up. When they arrived, they asked me to explain what I was experiencing—and whether they should call an ambulance. Without hesitation, I blurted out, "Oh God, no!" The only other words I could muster were, "Everything is just too real." I then handed my mom my copy of *Be Here Now* and said, "Maybe this will explain it." Needless to say, they weren't impressed.

 "Scream Phoenix" by Chris Grosso.
http://www.beyondword.com/indiespiritualist/
audiodownload8.m4a

25

TRANSMISSION OF THE HEART

*Whenever I see compassion, or real spiritual love,
I'm seeing in my environment the things that
I treasure in my soul.*

Ram Dass

There are numerous ways we can receive what I call the "transmission of the heart," many of which have already been written about in this book. But in my thirty-five years experiencing this thing we call life, that transmission has never been as clear, concise, or powerful as when I engulf myself in the teachings of spiritual icon Ram Dass.

Whether I'm reading one of his books, listening to his dharma talks, watching a documentary or Youtube video footage of him—every single time, without fail, my heart center ignites in a way that's virtually impossible to convey in words, save I had the writing skills of, say, someone like Thoreau, which unfortunately I do not.

What I can say is that it's an amazingly beautiful experience. It's a feeling of being whole, complete, and unconditionally loved, and that's no small feat—to feel completely and unconditionally loved—let alone by someone you've never personally met or spoken to. But that's what this spirituality thing is all about, finding that place of unconditional love, no matter what path, teachings, or lifestyle gets you there. For me, Ram Dass has been one of the great light-bearers guiding me back to that place of unconditional love, guiding me home.

It has always been a dream of mine to meet Ram Dass or even speak to him over the phone—*something, anything*, so I could thank him personally for all that he has done for me in my life.

In July 2013, I learned that he had a new book coming out, with Rameshwar Das, titled *Polishing the Mirror*, and I thought that could possibly be my chance. I'd been doing some successful interview segments with various spiritual teachers for the *Where Is My Guru* radio show, and figured that, if there was ever going to be a realistic chance of my speaking with him, this could be it. I knew when I sent the interview request that the chances were slim, as Ram Dass's health has kept him from doing much press in recent years. However, on the morning of July 10, I opened my email to a response from his longtime friend Raghu Markus, which read:

"Chris: Ram Dass can do a Skype interview with you on July 16 at 10 AM Maui time . . ."

And it was pretty much at that point that the tears began to fall as a result of the overwhelming love and gratitude I felt in my heart, a feeling that was almost too much to handle.

As I've already made clear, it's virtually impossible to convey the true effect that Ram Dass and his teachings have had on my life, but to know that I was going to have the opportunity to speak with him via a Skype video chat, as well as sneak in some of my gratitude before we got into the interview, well, it was just about the most surreal news I'd ever received. It was quite literally a dream come true.

I sat with those tears, in the humble awareness that I was being blessed with the opportunity to look Ram Dass in the eyes and share space with him, the man who's guided me deeper within myself, and closer to the true reality of who I am, than anyone else in my entire life.

Almost everything I talk about in this book can be traced back in one way or another to the effect Ram Dass's teachings (and an honorable mention to Ken Wilber) have had on me . . . and yet, I know that this is all greater than just one man—Richard Alpert, who blossomed into Ram Dass—just as it is greater than the physical manifestation of Maharaj-ji, Ram Dass's guru, who impacted (and still impacts) his life in such a profound way.

Contrary to how I'm writing about him in this piece, Ram Dass is not a god. And yet, he is an integral part of God, just as you and I are an integral part of God too. However, it takes illumined beings such as Ram Dass to guide the majority of us back to this realization, a realization that, when experienced, changes everything forever.

And so it is with gratitude, and in service, that I offer the following interview that I did with Ram Dass. He apologizes at the end for how slowly he spoke at certain times throughout our conversation, but I reassured him that the transmission of his heart still came through loud and clear. With that being said, I invite you to not only hear his words, but to also hear the teaching underneath his words. The gaps of silence not only offer passage for the transmission of the heart to come through, but also they invite us all to celebrate in a very real way Ram Dass's most beloved teaching, which is to simply *be here now* with what is.

 Watch the entire heartfelt interview with Ram Dass for the Where Is My Guru radio show. http://www.youtube.com/watch?v=O9Nt8JSSYfw

26

THIS LOVE

To be beautiful means to be yourself.
You don't need to be accepted by others.
You need to accept yourself.

Thich Nhat Hanh

Self-love seems to be one of the greatest struggles many of us face in our daily lives, and, trust me, I'm no exception. Many people base their self-worth on crazy ideas such as their weight, how many friends they have, or what kind of job they perform. Others base their sense of worth on how many sun salutations they do in a day, or how many things they've given away in the name of nonattachment, or how great they are because of whatever particular dietary lifestyle they choose. The unifying theme in all of this is that, for most, it never seems to be enough. We feel like we could always be doing something more—we could be skinnier, work at a more lucrative job, get rid of more stuff, or add an extra half hour to our yoga practice—but it's all in a vain attempt to fill some image of what we think we need to be in order to accept ourselves and be accepted by others.

We need to relax the ridiculous standards we set. And the way most of us mentally berate ourselves when we don't meet them—it has to stop. Ask yourself this question: "Would you speak to your friends and family half as harshly as you speak to yourself?" I mean, if your friends and family are assholes, that's one thing, but really, would you be as hard on them as you are on yourself, and if not, why not? Please take a moment to truly reflect on that.

Maybe you're one of the lucky few who consistently resides in a place of serene self-acceptance, and if that's the case I'm sincerely happy for you. The majority of us, however, well, we struggle with this a lot. For me, it actually got worse the more mindful I became. I started to become aware of some seriously self-judging and limiting thoughts, such as, "Well, you're looking extra fat today." "You really suck at playing the guitar and drums." "Man, you're ugly." "You don't have anything to offer this world, so why not go back to using drugs and drinking?" Those thoughts had been with me all along, but as my mind began to quiet through meditation practice, they now became much easier to hear. There seemed to be no end to them, and what made it worse was that, as those thoughts arose, I would then judge myself for having them . . . brilliant, right?

These thoughts and our internal mental struggles are truly the most unnecessary struggles we face in our daily lives, and it doesn't have to be that way. *Please* hear me right now when I tell you that you're so fucking perfect in your imperfections that it actually *is* funny.

you're so fucking perfect in your imperfections

I'm so serious when I say that. Our quirks—the things that we often look at with disgust—they are the things that make us unique and completely amazing! While that sentiment may sound like an after-school special to some, I wholeheartedly mean it. And I offer it directly from my heart, the heart that knows better than to take any of this mental ego chatter that tells us we're less than, seriously.

Fourteenth-century Tibetan master Longchenpa once said:

> Since everything is like an "apparition," Perfect in just being "What It Is"—as it is. Having nothing to do with "good" or "bad," "acceptance" or "rejection"—You might as well just burst out laughing![10]

And I've been blessed on more than a few occasions to have experienced what he meant by those words. Sure, the lovely shit storm that life can be will ultimately rear its ugly head from time to time, but as we learn to not take the self-defeating thoughts and mental chatter so seriously, and truly learn to embrace our perfectly imperfect selves, our lives become much more enjoyable.

I recently interviewed Jai Uttal (kirtan musician) after his performance at the *Yoga Journal* conference in Estes Park, Colorado, and while discussing a barrage of eclectic things, the topic of self-love came up. While I'm sorry that he too deals with the self-condemning mind, just like the rest of us, it was refreshing to hear someone in his position address the issue so candidly. Jai said:

Sometimes you can be with a group of people and feel so much love for them while you're looking around and then you get to yourself and you go, "Ugh." You like to skip over yourself real fast and go to the next person. It's a negative ego but only calling it ego doesn't help. I need to remember that I'm a human being too, so why can't I love me [*laughing*]? Last night, I did something, it was only the second time I did it and it's very silly, but it triggered something for me when I did it the first time last week. I was thanking all the performers who played with me and after I thanked them all, I looked down and said, "Thank you Jai." So I'm trying to be nice to me too. It's kind of childish, but it's work that needs to be done.[11]

"Why can't I love me?" Jai asks, which may be one of the most important questions any of us could ever ask ourselves. Many of us may think we love ourselves, but if we were to explore the stories our minds constantly feed us (often on such a deep level we're not even aware of them), you'd be surprised. For me, there was never any question about the lack of self-love, because it's always been clear as day. I've already shared some of my experiences that make that abundantly clear, but for others it's not always so obvious.

I had a profound yet very simple "aha" experience in meditation a few years back, and while it was nothing groundbreaking in the way of new spiritual revelations, it did change my entire life. As I sat on my nifty little zafu, failing miserably at calming my mind, I watched my haphazard thoughts begin to contemplate the wacky world of quantum physics. I'd been reading titles from Fred Alan Wolf, Amit Goswami, and others after watching the documentary *What the Bleep Do We Know?!* and was enthralled with the way physics and spirituality complement one another. So as I sat there thinking about quantum physics, and its assertion that all things at the level of both mind and matter are interconnected, thanks to atoms and their subatomic particles, a realization hit me, and it hit me hard. I realized that if we truly are interconnected, which, according to quantum mechanics (our most up-to-date science), we are, then everything, *everything*, including God, really is all One.

I began to think to myself, "Well, if God is in me, just as much as He/She/It is in the Buddha and Jesus, two solid dudes who instantly make my heart warm with feelings of love and compassion, why don't thoughts and emotions about myself create that same loving response?" And it all came full circle as I recognized ego to be the culprit. As I sat there with the understanding that it was my (ego) thoughts that were constantly nailing me to my own illusory cross, I also began to understand the complete bullshit nature of them, and that I didn't have to buy in to them anymore. That realization, understanding, and experience was such a relief!

So through that "aha" experience, I learned that self-love is much more than just liking my physical being and personality, because *real* self-love has very little to do with them. And as we begin to lay aside our attachment to those ideas, we allow a space for true self-love to reveal itself. It's a love of self that has no stipulations, which does not compromise, and cannot be swayed or tempered by our own (or others') thoughts and judgments.

27

TRIUMPHANT LIFE FUCK-UPS &
LOVING-KINDNESS

*Sometimes, to come to your senses,
you must go out of your mind.*

Alan Watts

I spent the greater part of my life not being beautiful, not being myself. I began getting pierced at sixteen and tattooed at eighteen, which was the earliest I legally could do so in my state. It was around junior high that I realized I didn't believe I, just as myself, was enough. I needed something more to make me feel special, or like I had something to offer. I know it probably sounds weird that something like piercings and tattoos made me feel that way, but they did. It wasn't long, however, before they failed to give me that false sense of self-confidence and worth they'd temporarily provided. (Note: I still get tattooed and am in no way against them. Today, however, I get them for different reasons.)

From piercings and tattoos, I moved on to drug and alcohol experimentation, abuse, and finally addiction. I have used, lied to, manipulated, and inflicted so much pain on family, friends, girlfriends, and strangers that, at times, it's almost unbearable to face.

I have spent the better part of my life not being beautiful, but I am not a victim and this isn't about writing for sympathy. This isn't some sappy, Hollywood story where things magically turn around and life becomes perfect after finding my way out of active addiction. You see, there's still very much a part of me that is rooted in the darkness of my past, and all the shit that's buried from years of selfish, self-destructive behavior. Sure, it's important to focus on the better things of today, but it's also highly irresponsible for me to ignore and pretend like the wreckage of the past isn't still taking up residence inside.

If I am to be truly responsible for myself, then I have to accept that discomfort and acknowledge the aspects of myself that scare the shit out of me and make my heart sink, because this is where true healing can begin.

I can tell you that, today, life is beautiful more often than not. I can say that. But I recognize that I'm only able to say that because I've spent a lot of time cultivating the qualities of loving-kindness and compassion for myself. It may seem selfish that I've worked on cultivating those qualities

wreckage of the past

first and foremost for myself, but I had to face the hard truth that, while I've always believed myself to be compassionate toward others (with the exception of my time in active addiction), the majority of it was a facade. I've never maliciously wanted to hurt others, even while using, but as much as I'd like to think that I've always wanted the best for them, if I was coming from a place where I didn't care about myself, how could I truly care for them?

If I really don't care about my own well-being, what does that say about my own mental state? If I really don't like myself, the self I base all my judgments and perceptions from, how then can I honestly, from the bottom of my heart, offer someone else compassion and loving-kindness? After looking very thoroughly at that, I can honestly say that, at least for me, it's not possible.

If I'm wishing others happiness, yet not including myself, who are my aspirations really helping? If I'm coming from a place of pain and suffering, of self-loathing, then how sincere can my loving-kindness and compassion be toward another? How can I give what I don't have in the first place?

Loving-kindness and self-compassion have been the most difficult areas for me to work with since I've embarked on the spiritual path, but I've come to recognize that they are absolutely essential. A big part of this recognition hit me hard one day while I was contemplating non-duality. This may sound ridiculously obvious and simple, but it really was a huge moment of clarity and remembrance for me.

As I sat, contemplating my interconnectedness to all beings, I began thinking about the people of whom I wasn't particularly fond, whether they were directly or indirectly in my life: acquaintances, family, politicians, conservatives, racists, sexists, homophobes. Then, laying my own judgments aside and focusing strictly on love, I extended loving-kindness to them all from the sincerest depths of my heart. Things all came crashing, however, when an image of myself appeared in my mind.

I immediately felt my body tense up as I shuddered back from the imagery. But then, this feeling was followed almost instantly by a sense of calm and deep recognition. I realized that, if I truly believed in the interconnectedness of all beings, and that at our core we're all love, then who was I to exclude myself?

How was it that, in my mind, the Divine's love was applicable to *everyone*, literally everyone, except me? If we really are all One, then who the hell am I to exempt myself from this love?!

I also realized that, when I'm condemning myself mentally for my past actions, on a deeper level, I'm condemning you too, and I don't want to live from that place of separation anymore.

"Hand of the Host" by Chris Grosso.
http://www.beyondword.com/indiespiritualist/
audiodownload9.m4a

28

EDEN COMPLEX

That wasn't any act of God.
That was an act of pure human fuckery.
Stephen King, The Stand

One of the dirtiest words today, both in and out of spirituality, is *God*, and in many cases rightfully so. The amount of blood spilled in the name of God is both sad and sickening. Aside from the wars fought over religious differences, there are also many more subtle (and not so subtle) divisions amongst people, precipitated by a "my God" versus "your God" mentality. When we draw these invisible lines in the sand, and keep ourselves separated from one another based on religious and spiritual beliefs, or a lack thereof, humanity's growth is crippled. Also, when we condemn one another for sexual preferences, political affiliations, forms of worship, and so forth, it keeps us stuck in a cycle of division and isolation. Today, however, many people are shedding these outdated paradigms and no longer living in fear of that old guy in the sky, supposedly keeping score with a furious vengeance.

Spirituality not only facilitates greater peace and calm in our lives, but also puts us in touch with something greater than ourselves. I'd like to emphasize the key words *greater than ourselves* and not *separate from ourselves*, as the old paradigm of searching outwardly is finally starting to dissolve. So how does one reconcile all of the dogma and nonsense that's been attached to God throughout the years, and begin to cultivate their own understanding and, more importantly, experience? A great place to start is in remembering that *God* is just a word. It's a huge injustice to try and box the magni-

God is just a word

tude of something like Christ Consciousness or Spirit, Buddha Nature or Brahman, into neat little packages so we can pretend like we've figured it all out.

Prior to exploring spirituality in my own life, I had trouble reconciling myself to the idea that there was someone greater at the helm than the egoic self I call Chris. It's not that I didn't believe it was true. In fact, I've always sort of had an internal knowing that it was real, but since most of my family and friends weren't into religion or spirituality, I didn't know where to begin in order to pursue and explore that eternal knowing.

Inevitably, it was through reading, and applying the various techniques and practices taught in the books I was devouring, as well as the meditation groups I would sit with, that I came to understand that the ultimate goal of any heart-centered spiritual practice is to reach a place where we leave the practices and teachings behind and reside in permanent connection with the One, or dare I say, *God*.

According to many Eastern philosophies, that state of being can take thousands of lifetimes to reach. It is even said that, in the moment the Buddha attained enlightenment, he was able to see the thousands of lifetimes he'd lived leading up to his awakening. There are those who believe that Jesus lived numerous lifetimes as well, before taking his final birth in which he became the Christ. I offer those examples not as a point of debate but rather to exemplify that this shit takes time. And in knowing that, it's important to have patience and reverence for the sacred path we've embarked upon and rest easy in the knowledge that, as long as we're spending time each day working with some sort of practice that facilitates a deeper understanding and experience of something greater than ourselves, then we're already well on our way.

You see, who we are beyond our physical body is enlightened right now in this very moment, because that's our natural state. The thing is, whether we point the finger at karma, conditioning, or ego, it's still the case that enlightenment has become a distant and faded memory (if even that) for the majority of us. But that's okay too. As we continue cultivating our practice, our awareness will naturally realign itself with our inherently enlightened state of being, our original state. And whether we fully reconnect with that state in five minutes, five years, or five lifetimes, *it will happen.*

29

GOD DISCLAIMER

To listen to some devout people,
one would imagine that God never laughs.

Sri Aurobindo

Whatever words you choose—Divine, Source, Spirit, Collective Consciousness, Higher Self, Life, Nature, The Force—my understanding and experience of God is very different than that of most traditional societies, and welcomes the agnostic and atheist as much as it does the Muslim, Hindu, Christian, Buddhist, Jew, and so forth.

My personal search has led me to resonate most deeply with the non-dualistic approach, which asserts that we're actually safe at home in the Godhead at this very moment, while experiencing a illusory nature of this day-to-day material world as it is projected from our mind (which is something quantum physics, our most contemporary and accurate form of science, supports). It's like when you acknowledge someone with the greeting *namaste*, which roughly translates to, "the Divinity within me recognizes the Divinity within you, and when we are in that place together, we are One Divinity."

A lot of people say namaste because it's a spiritually fashionable word, but never truly take into consideration its deepest implications, which, again, is pure non-duality. When we say namaste, we're literally telling another person that we recognize our imme-diate surroundings to be illusory and that, underneath all of it, at our core, there is absolutely no difference between us, or even between nature or any other physical thing that appears to be exist-ing for that matter. We're literally saying that it is all *One*. This non-dualistic "Oneness" is something that's virtually impossible to explain in words, however, and really must be experienced in order to be understood. (And in the Bonus Track section at the end of the book, I provide you with methods to facilitate this experience for yourself.)

Now, non-duality aside, we're still in this human existence on a daily basis, and it would be silly to try and pretend like we're not. So the way I've personally come to experience God within our material existence is as the orchestrating consciousness behind this entire show. It is not a singular man in the sky, smiting people left and right, but rather an intelligence that is as present in the cells of our bodies as it is in the farthest reaches of the cosmos. Similar to a mother, who holds her newborn in a state of pure love, this intel-ligence creates you, me, and this entire experience from a place of uncompromising love.

This God is incapable of understanding the judgmental nature that many religions have assigned to "Him," because all it knows *is* love (oh, and it's not a He or She either). But again, all of this—from non-duality to Collective Consciousness—is only *my* experience of God, and I'm not here to say that I'm right, or that, if you experi-ence God in another way, you're wrong. You may simply believe in the human spirit of goodness, without attributing it to any outside source (i.e., some type of god), and that is absolutely perfect too.

There are ways to begin cultivating a more serene and mindful way of living, regardless of whether you believe in God. We all have

God is incapable of understanding judgmental nature

this potential, and the potential to love ourselves and others in a deeper way, making our planet a more accepting and nurturing place to live. The God concept, left to man's dogmatic and old conditioned paradigms, has on many occasions put a strain on that progress, but I'm here to offer you some alternatives; ways in which we can all grow together, and respect and honor one another's life choices. It's all about moving onward and inward, my friends.

But as LeVar Burton used to say on *Reading Rainbow*, "You don't have to take my word for it." In that spirit, the following are a few selected excerpts from interviews I personally conducted with other Indie Spirits out there, to get their take:‡

"God is the most obvious thing in the world.
It's the rest of us whose existence I doubt."
—**Brad Warner**, Sōtō Zen priest, author, blogger,
documentarian, and punk rock bass guitarist

"You'll just have to ask Him or Her.
That's not a throwaway answer either.
I completely stand by the statement [*laughing*]."
—**Krishna Das**, Grammy-nominated kirtan musician

"It's really amazing what God can do.
Who would have ever thought I'd find
love, contentment, and joy in a prison cell, but I did."
—**Christian Hosoi**, professional skateboarder

"Most of our progress in science and philosophy has been
achieved by those who rebelled against 'God' and the Church,
or the dictates of conventional society."
—**Peter H. Gilmore**, high priest, Church of Satan

"Ok, listen . . . There is no significance of God in my life, God is my life. I would not be, without God. I am supposed to be dead. In 1968, I was in the hole going to the gas chamber, but there

was a divine intervention. And in knowing that, for me to get
upset, or be mad, or angry, is like slapping God in the face.
So here I am. I didn't make a deal with God, because you can't
make a deal with God. He put me here to talk to kids and to talk
to drunks and help addicts. The blessing that God has given me
is that when I walk on campus, I've already got their attention."
—**Danny Trejo**, actor, *Machete, Heat, The Devil's Rejects*

"God is still in the business of redemption."
—**Jamie Tworkowski**, founder of
To Write Love on Her Arms

"There is a causal agent that gives us a freedom of choice
to choose the really new stuff, creativity."
—**Amit Goswami**, theoretical nuclear physicist

"Trying to answer the question of whether God exists is
somewhat of an impossibility."
—**Dr. Andrew Newberg**, author and director of research at
the Myrna Brind Center of Integrative Medicine at
Thomas Jefferson University Hospital and Medical College

"There is absolutely nothing going on but God."
—**Andrew Harvey**, author and director of
The Institute for Sacred Activism

"What is most important is to have gratitude to be alive.
Everything is a gift from life, which is the same as that energy
source which some may call God."
—**don Jose Ruiz**, coauthor of *The Fifth Agreement*
with don Miguel Ruiz

"Yes, God exists—God is the air we breathe. God is . . ."
—**Miten**, spiritual musician

"I would say Godliness exists."
—**Deva Premal**, spiritual musician

"I don't give very much credence or value to belief systems . . .
but the mind says a lot of things, and most of the time it's pretty
transparent, but the heart knows, especially when we
allow ourselves to sink into it."
—**Jai Uttal**, Grammy-nominated kirtan musician

"I don't care what buildings you're worshipping under,
the bottom line is we're all worshipping the same one,
let's celebrate that."
—**Michael Berryman**, actor, *One Flew over the Cuckoo's Nest*,
The Hills Have Eyes

"Who we *think* God is doesn't exist because it (he or she) is a
creation of our conceptual thoughts.
I use the word God to point to life itself, which certainly exists."
—**Gangaji**, spiritual teacher

"I absolutely believe that God exists and for me
that means divine intelligence.
An intelligent presence or spirit that is the creator, maintainer,
even destroyer, as the Hindus may say, in life."
—**Marci Shimoff**, speaker and author

"I'm an atheist."
—**Scout Taylor-Compton**, actress, *The Runaways*,
Rob Zombie's *Halloween I* and *II*

---

‡ Read the interviews that these quotes came from—including my talks with Bernie
Siegel, Fred Alan Wolf, don Jose Ruiz, and more—at TheIndieSpiritualist.com.

30

INTELLECTUALIZE THIS

People never learn anything by being told;
they have to find out for themselves.

Paulo Coelho

Grammy-nominated kirtan musician Krishna Das once told me, "I don't believe in intellectual up-leveling, I believe in dealing with things as you experience them." And that was something I could immediately relate to.

You see, I'm not the best at retaining specific information. I mean, I read like it's going out of style—usually juggling anywhere from two to four books at a time—but I suck at memorizing and reciting the intricacies: specific sutras, aphorisms, verses, quotes, and so forth. It's been my experience, however, that the cores of these intricacies reside in our hearts, not our minds, so to understand these teachings experientially, instead of just intellectually, opens us up for deep transformations.

Still, I often find myself feeling inadequate, like I'll never know enough *stuff* to make my writing, speaking, or workshops worthwhile for others. I know that I'm committing a cardinal sin by admitting such a personal fear, especially in a "spiritual book," because, while I personally think it's bullshit, once you're published, it typically attaches some semblance of "authority" to your name.

But as far as I'm concerned, fuck that. I'm not going to pretend like I'm something I'm not. I'm as much a student (and teacher) as those of you who are reading these words, and the minute I start thinking otherwise, that's the moment I lose touch with my own humility. Zen Buddhists talk about "beginner's mind," which is an ideal place to be because it keeps us ripe for sharing and learning information with an open and inquisitive mind.

Knowledge on the path is always a good thing. Learning from those who came before us is an integral part of the process, but what good does said knowledge do if we only use it to boost our own ego, rather than to cultivate the experience(s) which the words themselves are pointing to? In his book *The Experience of Nothingness*, Sri Nisargadatta Maharaj said:

> If you discuss things with me, based on the traditional literature and the traditional knowledge . . . there will be so many pundits who are so knowledgeable they will eat me alive. And yet, where the basic knowledge is concerned, which is what I deal with, why do these people remain speechless?[12]

So sure, for example, you can tell someone all about a peach—what it looks like, smells like, tastes like—but until that person eats a peach for themselves, they'll never fully know its true nature. Personally, I'd rather just cut to the chase and bite into the goddamn peach than spend inordinate amounts of time conjecturing and hypothesizing about it.

So while I keep reading my books with highlighters in hand, usually forgetting most of the amazing intricacies I adorn in neon yellows, pinks, and blues, I *have* found that these forgotten gems have culminated into one great experiential teaching of the heart, from which I usually live, and I'll gladly recite that sermon all day long.

31

A DRUG IS A DRUG IS A DRUG

Love of love written by the broken hearted,
love of life written by the dead.

Mark Z. Danielewski, House of Leaves

Days, weeks, and months of pain, emptiness, and a general sense of all things awful turned into years before my very eyes. Emergency rooms, detoxes, rehabs, jail cells, and even psych hospitals became commonplace for me. I was living a hopeless existence, yet at the same time something inside of me, *deep* inside of me, would not give up. It definitely had nothing to do with my own self-will and is subsequently what I've come to know in years since as *God*. It did take a lot of pain and suffering for me to come to that understanding, however.

My personal addiction was, and is, narcotic drugs and alcohol, and they had begun taking their toll on my mental state. I had sunk into a dark depression and had begun cutting myself when I wasn't high, to feel something, anything. There was actually a phase in my life when I would spread a dozen sharp steak knives on my bed before lying down on them and going to sleep. The reality of my life had become such that that sort of darkness was eerily soothing to me. I spent many years not caring whether I lived or died, often hoping for death to come, twice even making

115

feeble attempts at killing myself. But my hopes and attempts were to no avail.

The first attempt was actually a double whammy, as I was already in a detox unit, going through withdrawals and miserable to my core. It was during my second day in detox, completely out of my mind from all the drugs I'd been pumping into my body, as well as the Ativan they were giving me (to keep me from having a seizure due to the amount of alcohol I'd been drinking), that I tried to take my life. It was a very feeble attempt. Early that morning, I checked out a shitty, disposable, double-blade razor from the desk, ostensibly to "shave" with, but knowing full well what I actually intended to use it for.

To my disappointment, though, after I broke out the blades, I saw how tiny and flimsy they were—hence why someone in a detox unit would be allowed to use the razor in the first place. I was a man on a mission, however, and began digging those flimsy blades as deep as I could into my wrists. I didn't know exactly where to cut, but I did remember hearing that the proper way was to cut vertically, not horizontally, as is often portrayed in the movies. So vertically I cut. There was much more blood than actual damage done, though, and my attempt was ultimately thwarted by one of the clinician assistants who came to check on me.

Within the hour, I was transported by ambulance to the emergency room of a nearby hospital, then back to the rehab facility to finish five more days of my detox, and, finally, back to the hospital's psych floor for seven days. That sort of shit was my reality back then, and I still have the ridiculous scars on my wrists. I could easily have them touched up by my tattoo artist, but have chosen to leave them there as a reminder of how dark my life once was, and how quickly I could slip (and unfortunately have) into old behaviors that would bring me back to that place.

The second attempt was definitely more sincere. It was the middle of the day and I was home drunk, which was commonplace for me at that time. It was one of my exceptionally dark periods, though, darker than my usual dark, and I just felt like I couldn't take it anymore. I had just refilled my prescription for Klonopin, which I was taking for an anxiety condition that existed purely as a result of my alcoholism. I was three-quarters of the way through a fifth of very cheap vodka when I decided to swallow the majority of the pills from my bottle.

As I sat there for a few moments after taking the pills, I remembered a time from junior high school when we had an impromptu assembly in our gymnasium, during which our principal notified us that a fellow student had died; he had committed suicide by drug overdose. This was a huge deal for our small community, because nothing like that had ever happened before. The part of this memory that stuck out to me the most, however, was that, in the days that followed, rumors spread about how the student was found. Supposedly when the medics arrived, he was still alive and crying. He knew that he was dying, and was regretting what he had done, telling the medics that he didn't want to die.

I never found out if there was any actual truth to that or if it was all just made-up rumor, but, for whatever reason, that memory, one which I hadn't thought of in many years, hit me like a ton of bricks, and I made the decision to call 911. After I made the call, I did not stay on the line like they asked, and I remember mentally berating myself, thinking I was a pussy for not being able to go through with it and what a fucking failure I was because I couldn't even commit to killing myself.

When the ambulance arrived, I was given some terrible coal-type drink. I was completely out of it and most of my memories from that point are a blur, but I'll never forget that awful goddamn drink. After a day or so in the emergency room, I again found myself in a short-term stay at mental hospital (I was very good at convincing them I was fine and that I just wanted attention, which was partially true). From there my life continued on this destructive path for many years.

There was no God as far as I was concerned, and spirituality was nothing more than a crutch for those not capable of being themselves. However, I was doing the same thing with my own drug addiction that I faulted religion and spirituality for. I was scared to be myself, and I masked that fear with drugs, the same kind of masking I'd mentally judged them for due to their belief in God.

Little did I know, however, that plenty of people in those religious and spiritual circles also struggled with similar addiction issues. But in my judgmental mind-set, I was unable to entertain the possibility that I could have anything in common with them.

Point in case, the wonderful kirtan musician Jai Uttal shared candidly with me about his own addiction struggles and the impact it's had on his life and spirituality:

> For me, I feel that my earliest use of drugs had a reason and a value, but I lost track of that completely. I was exploring my shadow side but then got lost in it and didn't know I was lost. I can go on and on about what I'd say the negative relationship of drugs is with the devotional path, I'm still learning though.
>
> I find on the path of bhakti [worship of the divine], blissful experiences are one of those nice side effects, but they're not the thing, they're not the big deal. They're just experiences, and when we take drugs, we begin to hook onto the experience and not the deeper longing to learn how to surrender and learn how to serve, to somehow set aside the ego. I used to have to alter myself all the time to feel that I was in the right place to sing. Part of that was incredible stage fright, but a part of it was also a certain belief that in my normal consciousness, I couldn't approach that space.
>
> Now however, I feel like every bit of my consciousness is put here by God and I have to accept that. It's not like I'm always in this bright light space, but I have to accept that if I feel that these blissful feelings can come from God, I also have to feel that the more mundane, or even "blue" feelings come from God too, and that whatever space I'm in is the appropriate moment for my devotional practice. I don't have to get high to feel devotional because that's fucked up, but again, I do feel like it's an individual thing."[13]

It's so important to really take to heart what Jai said about feeling blue, regardless of what mental and emotional space we find ourselves in, because *it is* always appropriate for our practice. That's been one of the hardest things I've come to accept and make peace with on my path. Today, I'm able to recognize the occasional dark times as being just as relevant to my path as those times when I'm feeling happy and everything is going great. As a matter of fact, I actually find that those have been the times that have deepened my practice the most, especially in regard to mindful acceptance and making peace with the present

When we stop ourselves from running away from the discomfort ... natural healing does occur

moment. When we stop ourselves from running away from the discomfort and instead compassionately allow it to play itself out, natural healing does occur. Oftentimes it's easier said than done, but it's absolutely doable nevertheless.

32

PILLS

*Help me to find a place where love
is not some half illusion.*

Wrench in the Works, "Dust Over Time Test"

There are plenty of things I did while in active addiction that I have absolutely no recollection of, and, at the risk of sounding irresponsible, I honestly believe that for the most part it's better that way. Unfortunately, the same can't be said for my family, who witnessed so much of the insanity (though, luckily, there's also much of it they didn't see).

Once in a very, *very* blue moon, my mother and I will talk about what it was like for each of us back when I was lost in the grips of addiction. It's definitely a rare occurrence, as the pain surrounding those times is very hard on the both of us.

There was one conversation we had several months ago, however, that was particularly painful for me. I should note that these rare conversations are always had in the spirit of healing, and in the celebration of a life that for all intents and purposes should have ended numerous times before, yet somehow miraculously made it through.

So as my mother and I talked, she shared about one of my blackout drunk episodes at their house and how my father had confiscated my bottle of Klonopin, because they knew that mixing the two could easily lead to either an overdose or me inflicting other kinds of harm on myself (this happened before, the time I did actually try to kill myself by mixing alcohol and Klonopin, which I've already shared about in this book).

My mother told me that, in a dire attempt to get my pills back, I pulled out a big kitchen knife from our drawer, went outside into our driveway, held it to my throat, and threatened to kill myself right then and there if my father didn't give them back to me. As my mother told me this, I began to feel sick in ways that I can only compare to my actual experiences of going through withdrawals themselves—nausea, anxiety, depression, an overall head-to-toe feeling of skin crawling, and basically just wanting to die.

I kept my composure, however, not letting on that anything was bothering me, because it would have never been my mother's intention for me to experience what I was going through as a result of what she was telling me, and I definitely didn't want to cause her any more pain than I already had. After our conversation, I went upstairs and took in everything she'd just told me. Besides the terrible sickness I was feeling, an overwhelming sadness began to set in as well. Fuck, to be completely honest, even as I'm writing these words right now, I'm aware of the haunting residual effects beginning to arise—but I digress, as there's a silver lining to all of this, which I'll get to shortly.

As I sat mindfully with the experience, I began to realize that there were two specific things that were the central cause of my pain. The first was a deep sorrow over the fact that I had lived my life like that, a life where something like holding a knife up to my throat was acceptable for me, regardless of how heavily under the influence I was. The second was that I had put my family through such horrific experiences, not only that one, but countless others, which in turn has left them with no shortage of painful memories to contend with.

an overwhelming sadness began to set in

Here's the silver lining to this otherwise gritty piece, however. As I sat there taking this all in, I realized that I had a decision to make. I could either stay on my pity pot, feeling bad for both myself and my family, or I could own it and work with it in a way that was conducive to healing.

In gratitude of this recognition, I chose the latter and mustered up the courage to continue truly looking at the experience I was having in that moment. I looked at the pain that I was experiencing because of what I'd put my family through, as well as accepted the fact that I had allowed myself to live in such a horrible way—mentally, emotionally, spiritually, and physically. As I sat, looking this experience directly in the face, I began to touch it with compassion.

I closed my eyes and practiced one of the Buddha's teachings on calming the body and mind. I held the pain with the same love and compassion with which a mother holds a crying newborn baby. I acknowledged the pain, accepting it for exactly what it was, and exactly how it had arisen in my experience. Then, I embraced it. I mentally told it that I was aware of its presence and that I would sit with it, keeping my heart open to it for as long as it needed.

I held the pain with the same love and compassion with which a mother holds a crying newborn baby

As my body and mind began to calm, I then looked into the cause of the pain, which was my previous actions and the subsequent pain and suffering they've caused both myself and my family. And finally, after sitting with the pain and allowing it to be exactly as it was for roughly an hour, I fully recognized and embraced that what is in the past is in the past, and there's absolutely nothing I can do to change it. However, by living the life that I do today, one in which I make integrally healthier choices while taking others' well-being into consideration at the same time, I'm now able to use my past actions as a catalyst to help both myself and others in the healing process. It's the inspiration that helps me give back whenever and however I can to those in need (including myself), and when I see it in that light, it's not quite as painful anymore.[§]

 "Cardboard Suitcase" by Chris Grosso.
http://www.beyondword.com/indiespiritualist/
audiodownload10.m4a

[§] Oh, and in the spirit of closure regarding the driveway incident: My dad gave me back the pills. I mean, what could he do? His son was standing before him, threatening to take his own life. Once I got the pills, I hightailed it out of there on foot, only for my parents to find me sitting in a grassy knoll, several miles away, a couple of hours later, and even further out of my mind . . . which ended in one of my ridiculously numerous trips to the emergency room. Shit like that always leaves me wondering why I made it through those experiences, and I'm still here, while so many other good friends I've known weren't as fortunate.

33

WHERE'S THE DEAD BODY!?

The Edge ... there is no honest way to explain it because the only people who really know where it is are the ones who have gone over.

Hunter S. Thompson

Meditation can be a hell of a thing, *especially* for those recovering from addiction or who've suffered a trauma of any kind. It has its own sneaky way of bringing shit up from our past that we believed long since gone.

As I sat in meditation recently, I had one of those experiences. It's something I've learned to laugh at now—the absolute ridiculousness of it is very Bukowski-esque—but there's of course a small part of my stomach that still knots up when memories like these rear their ugly heads.

This particular memory took place one winter evening circa mid-2000. I was drunk, like, really tying one on, when I decided to order a pizza for delivery. Usually, during my heavy drinking times, I could pretty much only eat when I was drunk, and for whatever reason I could usually only stomach shitty processed foods.

At the time, I was living in a basement apartment, which was part of a six-apartment house. In my inebriated state, I was feeling a bit cooped up, so I decided to wait for the delivery person on the front porch rather than in my apartment, which was located in the rear of the house. I ventured out and was making my way to the front of the house when I slipped on some ice in the driveway. Luckily, however, I regained my balance, which was no small feat for someone three sheets to the wind like I was.

I made my way to the front of the house, noticed that the street was relatively empty, and that was it . . . until I was startled awake in my bed by a cop, who was standing over me yelling, "Where's the dead body!?"

I sat up and everything was blurry. The complete shock of that cop yelling at me, followed by seeing roughly half a dozen police officers looking around my living room, did manage to temporarily sober me up a bit, but I was still totally shitfaced. I noticed that it was still dark outside and put two and two together that it was still the same night, but I had no recollection of what had happened up to that point.

I don't remember how I responded to any of the officer's questions—regarding dead bodies or otherwise—and my only other real memory of the experience was of being taken out of my apartment on a stretcher by paramedics. It was a real scene: an ambulance, fire truck, multiple patrol cars, lights flashing everywhere. My neighbors stood in the driveway, taking it all in, including a supervisor and co-worker who just happened to be driving by (my job at the time was located less than a minute from where I lived, at the end of my street).

I woke up the next morning in the hospital, feeling a special kind of shit-tastic. I was still drunk, but not drunk enough to mask the nausea or the pain that engulfed the majority of my body. The

a special kind of shit-tastic

hospital psychologist eventually made her way in to see me, and that's when I found out what had brought the police to my apartment in the first place.

So it goes like this: The delivery guy arrived with my pizza and called my cell to let me know he was out front. After two unanswered calls (per checking my cell history the next day), he drove around back to my apartment door, which I'd apparently left about halfway open.

My apartment was very small, so tight that everything—the kitchen, living room, my bedroom—could basically be seen from the entrance. So apparently the delivery guy got quite the surprise when he poked his head into my half-open door and saw a big puddle of blood on the kitchen floor, and what he thought was my dead body (complete with a bloody face and everything) sprawled out on my bed. He immediately proceeded to call 911 and report what he thought may have been a dead body, relaying that I wasn't responding to anything he said to me.‖

Once my blood alcohol content dropped below .08, the legal limit in Connecticut, I was released from the hospital. I didn't call anyone for a ride. It was only a three-mile walk, so I went for it, though it was a tough three miles; besides the hangover, which was in full effect, my head was throbbing and my belt had gotten lost somewhere in the mix, so I had to hold my pants up the entire walk home (I prefer to wear pants that are one size bigger than my waistline, because, I don't know, I just do).

When I got back to the apartment, the first thing I saw was the bloodstain on the tile floor, which was basically dry at this point. I wasn't fazed in the least. I proceeded to open the cabinet next to the blood, which is where I'd often leave my alcohol, in the hopes that there was still some in there—and *hallelujah*, there was. Enough at least to get me drunk-ish, which would allow me to shower before heading out to the store to get more liquor to sustain myself for the day.

I walked over to the couch with the jug of vodka in hand, sat down, and looked back over at the puddle of blood. I laughed an insane "fuck you, death" kind of laugh. The kind that told death I'd won again . . . at least this time.

I then glanced down at the coffee table in front of me and saw my copy of the Bhagavad Gita and Narcotics Anonymous Basic Text both sitting there. My laugh subsided for a brief moment, as did the insanity. I became aware of how fucking crazy of an experience I'd just gone through . . . but that moment of clarity was short lived, as I was nowhere near ready to face the magnitude of it. So I smiled a crooked and painful smile, raised my jug of vodka in the direction of the Gita and Basic Text in a taunting sort of way, and I drank deeply. So deeply that, when I stopped, it was only because I had to take a deep breath.

Returning to present day, as I came out of meditation and the memory of this experience, I stopped and breathed deeply; however, this breath was accompanied by serenity rather than vodka. I then looked over to my bookshelf where I still have those copies of the Gita and Basic Text, and smiled at them. This time, however, my smile was one of heartfelt gratitude rather than insane mockery. It was a smile of appreciation to be living a life that once was lost, but that today, just for today, is found.

‖ I later retraced my steps, and what it looks like happened was that I slipped on the stairs on the front porch, banging my head on one of them as I fell, which caused a cut on my forehead (there was a little blood on one of the stairs and some random spots on the snow/ice leading back to my apartment). Once I arrived back at my apartment, I must have stopped when I entered the kitchen, leaning against the counter with my head hanging down, blood dripping onto the floor. After standing like that for a few moments or so, however long it took to make the puddle, I made my way to the bedroom to lie down, and the rest is history. Well, at least that's my personal sleuthing conclusion, anyway.

34

A PRAYER FOR THE DEAD

It is no measure of good health to be well-adjusted to a profoundly sick society.

Jiddu Krishnamurti

I'd just finished playing my guitar when I glanced over at my computer screen and saw a picture of a bloodstained sidewalk on my Facebook feed. The caption beneath the picture read "Boston Marathon Bombing," and immediately I felt my stomach begin to twist as my thoughts turned to my uncle, who was running in the race that day, as well as my other family members who were there to support him. The reports about what had happened, the number of injuries and so forth, were still vague at best. I would later hear about my uncle's experience.

After crossing the finish line, he began the process of trying to walk off a 26.2 mile run and found himself needing to stop for a moment. He bent over, putting his hands on his knees in an attempt to recuperate his heartbeat and sense. As he stood back up seconds later, he faced west, looking for his family members who were there in support of him, when it happened—the first bomb went off.

A few seconds passed before the shock and confusion of the crowd was interrupted by another explosion, this time louder and stronger than the first. The crowd's confusion now turning to screaming cries of anguish and pain.

When all was said and done, three people were killed and over two hundred injured, yet my uncle (only slightly injured when his foot was hit with a small pellet from the bomb) and the rest of my family were safe. Needless to say, this was very emotional for all of them. In my uncle's own words: "I completed the Boston Marathon, but I never really finished . . . in some ways I left that part of my heart there on Boylston, in front of the Old South Church."

As the week went on, two brothers were named as suspects, and the typical pro-America, "don't fuck with us" mentality began to set in. One of the brothers was killed trying to escape authorities only four days after the bombing, while the other brother was captured. Pictures of the deceased older brother's body began littering the feeds on my social media networks, celebrating his death. There were also pictures posted of the younger, captured brother; his pictures, however, were accompanied by comments regarding raping, murdering, and torturing him as revenge. These were sentiments I found eerily reminiscent of the hate rhetoric that emerged toward Muslims following the 9/11 attacks in 2001.

So much anger, hate, and bloodlust left me asking myself, have we still learned nothing from our past? It was as if people were spitting in the face of Gandhi, essentially calling him a pussy for trying to teach us things like "an eye for an eye makes the whole world blind." But I suppose, fuck that, right? If somebody fucks with us, well, we're gonna fuck with them, right? Shock and awe, baby . . . Shock. And. Awe. We have to let them know who's boss, show them who they're really fucking with. We have to let them know who *really* runs shit around here, right?

The thing is, though, shit's not being run around here, or there, or anywhere else, because it's all completely out of control. And not just on a global or governmental level (because that goes without saying), but more importantly on a personal level. Think about this: If we're calling for justice through violence, are we really in control of ourselves, of our mental and emotional well-being? If we really want to harm someone else, how can we say we're in control? I'm not asking you to lie to yourself and pretend like you don't want to harm someone else if that's how you feel, but what I *am* asking you to do is not kid yourself and pretend like you *are* in control while feeling that way.

When we go to war and kill others, or take to the streets and beat people for revenge, no matter *what* the cause, there is no control in that. And it's not just Western culture, America, it's the majority of this fucked-up world that pits violence against violence as a means of finding bloodstained solutions to problems that can never be truly resolved in such a way.

finding bloodstained solutions

The greater part of humanity lives from a place where this sort of behavior is acceptable, both personally *and* globally, and I can't help but keep asking myself how murder, beatings, torture—any of it—is acceptable. How did we fall so far off as a species that we're okay with any of this?

And please, please don't tell me it's the real world and that I need to wake up, because that's the exact rhetoric they want you to believe. And once you do, they've enlisted you too.

35

DEATH, IT'S NOT JUST
for Metal Anymore

You don't know what death is!
Dr. Loomis, Halloween II (1981 version)

Most of us have thought about dying at some point or other. The contemplation of what happens after we've "crossed over" and no longer exist in this world can be a scary thought, especially because it's completely counterintuitive to how our minds typically process thoughts and information—which is to say, based on concrete, material, and tangible examples and explanations.

Death, however, completely shatters the safety of our day-to-day thought processes. Once we've laid aside our physical bodies, it's over; we're out of the equation altogether. I mean, I get it, who really wants to think about life without themselves in it (how's that for ego nature?). But the reality is that life goes on, even without us in it. Life happens before, during, and after our short time here on earth, so to ignore the inevitable—that no matter what, we're all going to die—leaves us vulnerable to all sorts of unnecessary pain and suffering.

The fear of death is the be-all, end-all fear, because well shit, *it's death* . . . it's the end of who most of us typically identify ourselves as (physical bodies). So when we tuck those thoughts and fears into our unconscious, our lives are built on a foundation of perpetual

fear—the fear of death. Many who read that last sentence will probably think to themselves: "That's not me. I'm happy and not afraid
of death." Sure, at face value, your everyday life, for all intents and
purposes, probably does seem like it's fine and that death doesn't
need to have any part in that equation, especially for the young (and
young at heart).

That being said, some might be asking themselves: "Well, if
everything is cool, then why should I care?" The answer is very simple. These hidden thoughts and fears play an integral role in our life.
So even though we've hidden them safely away in the back of our
mind, they're *still* there, regardless of whether we're aware of them.

I mean, really think about death for a moment—your death.
Picture yourself six feet under and no longer existing in this material realm. Now picture your body five years after your burial. You're
decomposing, and there are bugs crawling all over you. I know it's
gross, but it's reality (unless, of course, you get cremated). So I'm
guessing chances are better than not that, for most of us, if you really
did sit with those thoughts and images, you're probably left feeling a
bit uneasy. Those unpleasant feelings you're now consciously aware of
are a part of your everyday reality; they're just hidden well below the
surface. They are always there—the fearful thoughts and subsequent
uneasiness they create—but you can begin to release them if you're
willing to make a little effort. This can be an important opportunity
because, if we wait until we're facing death to give it our consideration, it will most likely be too late to truly process and make peace
with what is happening to us. As Sogyal Rinpoche, in his book *The
Tibetan Book of Living and Dying*, uncompromisingly states:

> To follow the path of wisdom has never been more urgent
> or more difficult . . . [But] the entire society in which we
> live seems to negate the very idea of sacredness or eternal
> meaning. So at the time of our most acute danger, when our
> very future is in doubt, we as human beings find ourselves
> at our most bewildered, and trapped in a nightmare of our
> own creation.[14]

Rinpoche is talking about a society dedicated almost entirely to the celebration of ego, "the nightmare of our own creation." We can alleviate that nightmare, however, and liberate ourselves from the impact this underlying fear of death has on our lives, if we begin to face and explore it now.

There is no shortage of conjecture surrounding death, what it means, why it happens, and what happens afterward, so if you're not sure where to start in your own exploration of this unnecessarily frightening topic, why not start by checking out what the various schools of spirituality have to say about it. Heaven and hell realms, karma and reincarnation, alternate universes, different astral planes of existence, the bardo, akashic records . . . there are really so many places you could go on your journey into the unknown. Or fuck it, if you'd like to get really personal about it, you could go hang out in a graveyard for a few hours and mindfully take that all in. Think about what's going on in the ground underneath your feet, read the tombstones and so forth.

death is going to come calling

We never know when death is going to come calling, so why not begin exploring what that experience may personally mean for you now, rather than later?

36

THE ENTANGLEMENT THEORY OF KIRTAN, PUNK ROCK & HIP-HOP

*If I should ever die, God forbid, let this be my epitaph:
The Only Proof He Needed for the Existence of God
Was Music.*

Kurt Vonnegut

Virtually all styles of music, whether traditionally spiritual or not, offer us the opportunity to visit deeper places within ourselves. To be completely honest, most traditionally "spiritual" music has typically done very little for me. I found my spiritual hymns in the ambient songs of bands like Sigur Rós, Múm, My Bloody Valentine, and Explosions in the Sky, or even heavier drone bands like Neurosis, Earth, and Isis. In retrospect, I now understand that these bands and songs often produce in me the same transcendent experiences I've occasionally heard others talk about having while listening to traditionally spiritual music.

Oftentimes while listening to the aforementioned bands, and many others, I found I could easily let go of the strict identification I placed on this material body that I typically consider the be-all, end-all reality of my experience. As I lost myself in their songs, they guided me to a place that transcended thought, a place where all that was left was the song of life **the song of life and death** and death, until even that disappeared and nothing but the music remained.

Those were my musically spiritual experiences for much of my younger life, and certainly still continue to be to this day. I did, however, eventually come across a form of traditional spiritual music that I fell in love with instantaneously. It's called kirtan.

My introduction to kirtan came when I listened to a CD that I'd taken out of my local library, by renowned kirtan musician Krishna Das, former lead singer of the legendary band Blue Öyster Cult (pre "(Don't Fear) The Reaper" era, unfortunately). I don't recall exactly how I first heard of Krishna Das, though it was probably through one of Ram Dass's talks or books, but I do remember honestly not being very optimistic about what I was going to hear once I pressed play. However, the moment I heard his harmonium (an air-driven instrument similar to an organ), I felt a sense of warmth begin to stir in my heart center—a warmth that still arises to this day whenever I listen to his music, and that of many other kirtan musicians.

I didn't know much about the words Krishna Das was singing, because they were in Sanskrit (an ancient language of India), but I could feel they were coming from a sincerely devotional heart, and that was good enough for me. The interesting thing is that the experience actually reminded me quite a bit of my earlier introduction to punk/hardcore and how moved I was when I heard the raw passion of singers from bands like Drive Like Jehu, Quicksand, and Hot Water Music. The same could also be said of my experience when I began getting into hip-hop and hearing the authentic soul behind emcees such as Nas,

they were all truths that resonated with me

Posdnuos from De La Soul, Vast Aire and Vordul Mega from Cannibal Ox, and KRS-One. And so I've come to realize that regardless of the style of music any of these artists were performing, whether punk/hardcore, hip-hop, or kirtan, they were all speaking their truth, and they were all truths that resonated with me.

In kirtan, there is a call-and-response element, which invites the listener to participate with the musicians while they're performing. The artist will sing a chant, which is the "call," and the audience will sing the chant back to them, which is the "response." This is not entirely unlike hip-hop artists or punk/hardcore bands who encourage their audiences to do the same. Kirtan differs, however, in that it's specifically a devotional type of music, aimed at guiding listeners or audience participants to a deeper experience of the Divine within themselves.

And while I also definitely appreciate the deeper connection I feel when singing along at a punk/hardcore, hip-hop, or metal show, I'm not going to kid myself and pretend that I'm singing praises to the Divine while shouting lyrics to "Angel of Death." But that's totally cool too. There's a time and place for all the things that resonate within us. Personally, I can rock out to Slayer, smiling at the entertainment aspect of it, and still be mindful that for me that's all it is: entertainment. And it's with continued spiritual practice that I've literally found myself at a Slayer concert, having a blast, while periodically just looking around at the audience and sending them **all that's left is the Divine itself** all love, because I knew that underneath the appearances and the music, we were still all One and it was still all love. Yes, even at a Slayer concert this type of awareness is possible.

Kirtan is obviously an entirely different scene, though. No sweaty dudes moshing into one another or women in super revealing clothing, unless they've just come from a yoga class (zing). In kirtan, we come together to chant and share a sacred space with others for a few hours, which often leads us to a place where there is no more *us* or *them*, and all that's left is the Divine itself.

As I hope I've already made clear, kirtan is *not* the only form of spiritual music capable of producing these transcendent experiences for people. As I've tried to exemplify, it's as possible for it to happen with nontraditionally spiritual music as it is with traditionally spiritual music. So here's to Krishna Das and Isis, Nas, Jai Uttal, Rakim, Sigur Rós, Neurosis, MC Yogi, Big L, Mogwai, Guru, and the countless other artists, bands, musicians, and emcees of the world who have provided me with the spiritual soundtrack to my life.

To give you a little taste of kirtan, here's a YouTube link of me and the wonderfully gifted yoga instructor Alanna Kaivalya playing at Kripalu. https://www.youtube.com/watch?feature=player_embedded+v=SUsuGGjhWsU.

37

MUSIC, THE COLLECTIVE
Liberator

When I hear music, I fear no danger.
I am invulnerable. I see no foe.
I am related to the earliest times, and to the latest.

Henry David Thoreau

Recently, while speaking with *New York Times* bestselling author Dr. Lissa Rankin about her appreciation of music, I found myself very moved by how beautifully she conveyed the impact it has had on her:

> Just as feelings sometimes don't feel real until I write them down, songs give voice to feelings I have trouble accessing until someone else gives them life. Hearing the lyrics of my life set to music somehow bypasses my brain, bee-lining straight for my heart and allowing me to experience the feeling without thinking about it. All that medical training that taught me to numb and stuff down my feelings so I could keep working through traumas did a number on me, but music liberates me from that numbing influence, helping me fully experience life's fully human emotions. Music also reminds me that the emotions we experience, which often feel so personal, are collective. This reminder of how

connected we are as divine sparks spun together like a web alleviates the loneliness I sometimes feel.[15]

This statement of Lissa's resonated deeply with me: "Hearing the lyrics of my life set to music somehow bypasses my brain, bee-lining straight for my heart and allowing me to experience the feeling without thinking about it." And it doesn't matter what type of music elicits that experience for you. Plenty of "heavier" music—particularly what's categorized as sludge, stoner, or doom—often impacts me in a way that I lose myself in meditative states, as their riffs play on and on in an almost pulsating way, a way that anchors me into a place where it's just the huge fucking riff accompanied by thunderous drums, bass, and nothing else.

These experiences are similar to the one I had at the Van Halen concert, just on a smaller scale. In the beginning, before I was into spirituality, I had nothing to compare with. I just knew the music was connecting me to something deeper than myself, something that now, with spiritual direction, I've come to recognize as a form of Collective Consciousness. It is both inside of us, and much greater than us, all at the same time.

I've been recording and touring with bands since the age of fifteen, and some of those experiences have been the most cathartic, healing, and unifying experiences of my life. Being on stage and connecting with people in the audience who are moved by your songs, whether it's by grabbing the microphone to scream along with the lyrics, or a good old-fashioned stage dive, is an amazing feeling. Hell, even if it's a stranger air-drumming along at a concert, that person is still connecting with the Collective Consciousness in their own way. It's all very communal, really. From hardcore to kirtan and everything in between, it's passion, it's a connection to something greater, it's a release, it's healing.

Collective Consciousness

Whether I'm playing a club with my doom band, Womb of the Desert Sun, or I'm performing kirtan at a yoga studio, it's all equally passionate and meaningful for me, because it's all coming from my heart. So whether I'm working on music and lyrics that are darker in nature, or drumming along to a beautiful harmonium while singing praises to Krishna, Kali, and Ganesh, it's all part of a healing process, and part of reconnecting myself to the Divinity housed within my heart.

As music flows through our bodies, it can guide us back to our natural state of being, a place where our mental constructs begin to quiet, allowing the Divine to become much more central in our awareness. We heal and grow spiritually by spending time in this place of connectivity, and through the music we enjoy.

38

BHAKTI BOOMBOX

Be true to yourself and you will never fall.
Beastie Boys, "Pass the Mic"

The idea of *indie spirituality* attempts to make all of the ideas and concepts shared in this book, "spiritual" or not, more accessible for those of us who've previously had a tough time with them. This isn't a new spirituality, but rather all spirituality. It is not exclusive to any person, sect, religion, race, sexual identity, or creed. It simply is. It is right here, right now, and it's all good, even when it's not. While speaking with MC Yogi, he did a wonderful job of elaborating on this point when he said:

> Once you've discovered who you are and what this all is, it doesn't matter where or who you are. There are saints in India who meditate on huge piles of trash. It doesn't matter what it looks like on the outside. It's all about being able to feel that which is beyond the senses, that point where the senses emanate and shine from within our self, the center of the wheel, clock, compass, mind, heart, whatever you want to call it. Our innermost point is there, the center of our universe. It's so important to be able to find that blazing sun

that is in the center of our self and return to it quickly, so that when the mind kicks up all of its ideas, which it does because it's designed like a machine to do so, we can detach from our ideas of how we think it should be and continue to return to the center.

In yoga there's a beautiful saying that "it shines through you as you." It takes the form of everything, but if we're slightly off center, then we're going to think it needs to look a certain way.[16]

The importance of being able to "detach from our ideas of how we think it should be and continue to return to the center" cannot be stressed enough if we want to truly remain open in our journey and able to honor the truth in ourselves while allowing others to do the same. Even if they aren't as accepting of what resonates with us, or our own personal life choices, we will be rooted in a place where, like Yogi says, "the senses emanate and shine from within our self, the center of the wheel, clock, compass, mind, heart." That's a place where a lot of people—including spiritual practitioners, unfortunately—don't come from. Yogi also went on to say:

I really struggle with that as an artist because I always feel like my art should look and sound a certain way. I always strive for perfection. It's very humbling and a constant reminder to return to center. When you align yourself, everything on the outside starts to fall into place. It's that shift, like when you go sailing, you make a tiny little course correction, a subtle little shift but it alters your course extremely. It's a tiny little internal shift, just like turning a key in a lock, sinking the mind back into the center, dropping in, you can't even see it from the outside.

That tiny little shift, however, radically changes your perception so you can actually see that everything is love in disguise. Everything is yourself in disguise and the personality is just the costume the Self wears. It's like the mind is a mask, a facade. What is behind the mind, below the breath, what is shining through the senses, what is seeing itself through you? The universe sees itself through our eyes. The universe is shining through our nervous system and to have this perspective takes work, it takes effort. There's a lot of conditioning that needs to be stripped away. You have to train your mind diligently in order to have that sort of breakthrough where you can shine through your own thoughts and become intimate with the infinite, which is shining in, and all around us. I love what Noah [Levine] is doing because he's shattering the idea that it has to look a certain way and I feel like that's spiritual maturity, when you can see it in everything, even in the fucked up situations too. If you can see that a great power is orchestrating that as well, in order for us to have that remembrance, it's strong medicine. It can be very bitter at times but if you're into the experience of being illuminated, then you just kind of relish and savor every square inch of it.[17]

Yogi really nails it when he mentions the tiny little internal shift that, even though we can't see it, radically changes our perception, allowing us to see that everything is in disguise. On the material level, it's all just image and stuff, and we too are spiritual aspirants regardless of what we've previously been told by traditional society and spirituality. It's our insides, not our outsides, that guide us on our paths, and we're full of heart, aren't we?

everything is in disguise

39

IGNITION

Say "Nevermore," said Shadow.
"Fuck You," said the Raven.

Neil Gaiman, American Gods

A sadness wells up inside of me. No rhyme or reason. I sit down, cross my legs, place my hands in my lap, and close my eyes. I sit with this sadness—both personal and impersonal—and hold the pain in my heart.

I sit with this sadness as an offering to anyone who is struggling. I know what it means to struggle, to experience pain and sadness. I know it intimately.

I sit with this sadness and, as I do, it acknowledges my presence. It knows I'm neither judging nor asking it to leave. Rather, I just simply want to be with it in the moment.

The sadness becomes awareness, and a sense of compassion begins to arise.

It sees that I need it, so the sadness slowly begins to fill my heart with warmth. The cells in my hands ignite with a tingling sensation that slowly moves simultaneously up my arms, into my chest, throat, and head, as well as down into my stomach, legs, and feet.

The sadness is still there, but it's much quieter now. It knows that I'm there with it, my arms and heart completely open to it.

The cells of my entire body continue to tingle until, finally, they merge into one unified sensation of soft and warm static energy. A faint angelic voice begins to sing within me. *In your love, my salvation lies in your love, my salvation lies in your love.* She repeats these words over and over and over again.

The warmth of my heart center turns into a smoldering fire that engulfs the remaining consciousness of my bodily experience— everything else, gone. And the angel continues to sing. *In your love, my salvation lies in your love, my salvation lies in your love.*

Eventually, her voice begins to fade, and my eyes slowly make their way open. I look around the room and see that everything is exactly as I'd left it, except that now the sadness has taken leave.

I smile at myself in the understanding that grace and grit—they're just two sides of the same coin, both equally beautiful, and completely ridiculous in their own right. *Cracking the facade. Ignition.*

 "The Last Night of the Earth" by Chris Grosso. http://www.beyondword.com/indiespiritualist/audiodownloadlll.m4a

40

VARIATIONS ON A THEME

We shall not cease from exploration
And the end of all our exploring
Will be to arrive where we started
And know the place for the first time.

T. S. Eliot

And so here we are, at the gates and ready to step through into a new paradigm, knowing that the deepest changes that take place in our lives are often those on the inside rather than out. And when we are no longer content to live a life conditioned by fear, resentment, blame, and judgment, when we lay aside preconceptions based on separation, when we allow space for the Collective Consciousness and acceptance of all beings, regardless of appearances, together we move forward. We clean our side of the street, and hell, we even help clean our neighbor's side as well. We do this by simply allowing them to be whoever they choose to be, placing no judgments on them, even if they're not willing to return the favor. Today, we no longer allow others to dictate our internal sense of well-being, not because we're better than anyone else, but simply stated, we're just fucking over it.

We also now see beyond what meets the naked eye, knowing that our old futile search for relief in strictly material pleasures will no longer cut it. Sure, we're bound to still get wrapped up in them from time to time, but now we're mindful of their fleeting nature and understand that the true sense of peace and comfort that we've been looking for can only *truly* be found within. The empty hole that many of us have experienced in our hearts is now being filled in a sincere and lasting way as we cultivate our relationship with the One interconnected source of love we all have in common.

We are now very clear that spirituality does not *strictly* have to do only with things like formally sitting on meditation cushions or spending a certain amount of time in prayer and so forth. Nor do we have to change our entire lifestyles around and become active members of traditional spiritual and religious groups if we don't want to, because we now understand that spirit is in *all things* at *all times*.

Let me be unequivocally clear when I say that meditation, prayer, and spiritual groups can all be wonderful things, if they're what resonates with you. But now we can also recognize that something as simple as hugging a friend, spending time with your family, going to a concert, jogging, or any number of various interests are all spiritual activities that will facilitate growth when done with even a hint of mindfulness. And as we continue to cultivate mindfulness, and deepen our awareness of the Divine within, through both formal and informal practices, everything becomes a spiritual practice—*everything*.

" Rising/Falling " by Chris Grosso.
http://www.beyondword.com/indiespiritualist/
audiodownload12.m4a

41

LOVE, THE UNIVERSAL
Curriculum

Yesterday we obeyed kings and
bent our necks before emperors.
But today we kneel only to truth,
follow only beauty, and obey only love.

Kahlil Gibran

L ife is not always going to be pretty. The human experience is
beautiful, terrifying, and very, very weird. But like the brilliant
author Hunter S. Thompson once said, "When the going gets weird,
the weird turn pro." So are you up for it? Are you ready to embrace the
beauty, terror, and weirdness, exactly as it is? Are you willing to be
vulnerable, live and love fearlessly, and celebrate our social, spiritual,
and cultural differences with a spirit of unity? If so, your life is about to
become more meaningful than you could have ever imagined.

This might sound corny, but, shit, I'm going to say it anyway. You
and I, we're brothers and sisters in this thing we call life. It doesn't
matter if you're Christian, Buddhist, white, black, Wiccan, atheist,
Chinese, Canadian, tall, short, tattooed, conservative, or whatever
else. *We are all* human. We all hurt and feel pain, and we know how
much that sucks, so why continue to inflict it on others due to petty
lifestyle or belief differences? Right now in this very moment, you
are capable of making the decision to let your heart be your guide. In
choosing so, you choose healing for all, because our heart will never
guide us toward harm of self or others.

We're goddamn brilliant beings

We're goddamn brilliant beings, all of us, and we're all capable of so many amazing things. You! Yes, you reading these words right now, you are amazing. I don't care that I've probably never met you. I still know that you're absolutely amazing. In this very moment, you're a conscious, living and breathing being, and that's absolutely fucking mind-blowing! You're forged from the very same consciousness that created the earth, the stars, and all the galaxies in the entire universe, and if that doesn't impress you, then I don't know what the fuck will.

As for me, I'm done taking this amazing experience of life for granted. From this day forward, I vow to do my best to live to the fullest the following words from the brilliant madman Charles Bukowski: "We are here to laugh at the odds and live our lives so well that Death will tremble to take us."

So, what are you waiting for? Let's get on with it, shall we . . .

Capping off the set the same way we started, here's a song from my band Womb of the Desert Sun, called "Transistor," from our EP Where Moths Eat and Worms Destroy.
http://www.beyondword.com/indiespiritualist/audiodownload13.m4a

Side B

DEMONS OF LIGHT

(Meditations, Practices, and Eclectic Multimedia Suggestions)

Meditations

Many teachers and scholarly types divide meditation into two categories, *concentration* and *awareness*, and from there it gets even more specific with a variety of subcategories, including, but definitely not limited to, *mantra*, *visualization*, and *koan* (to name only a few).

Contrary to popular belief however, meditation does not just happen in these formal practices. Formally sitting on a zafu (meditation cushion) with legs crossed and hands in a mudra (hand positions) is definitely a great place to start, but the important thing is—whether it's formally sitting, walking, visualization, or any other of the numerous methods available—we find the style(s) that feel right for us.

Honestly, I've found that anytime I bring mindfulness into my daily life, whether it's performing or listening to music, jogging, skateboarding, or whatever, it's all just as valid as any of the more "traditional" meditation practices. Really, when all is said and done, the goal and end result is going to be the same—to calm our discursive mind and open ourselves up to higher dimensions of awareness (not to sound all woo-woo or anything), and only we can know what feels right for us.

So remember, it's like what Noah Levine said in the foreword, "Try it for yourself, and trust your own direct experience. If the path that you are on leads to suffering and confusion, abandon it. If the path that you are on leads to freedom and well-being, follow it to the end."

1

VIPASSANA MEDITATION

Besides being asked, "What's an Indie Spiritualist?" the second most common question I'm typically asked is "What type of meditation do you practice?"

While I personally practice many different types of meditation—never feeling like I have to stay within the confines of only one tradition—I typically respond with *vipassana*, as I've found it to be the most universally applicable form of meditation around. Any form of meditation that resonates with you, however—whether guided, mantra, movement, and so forth—will definitely be of benefit.

I adore meditation because there are countless ways to meditate, with no particular style being any better than another. It's all about what resonates with *you*. You can find many free guided meditations online by searching Google or Youtube, as well as by visiting your local library. *Most* meditation practices are to spirituality what Bob Ross was to painting—very laid back and go with the flow. And while your practice may not provide you with happy little trees, it will over time create a greater sense of peace, clarity, and serenity in your life, and that's sorta like happy little trees, right?

Through years of drug addiction, I did considerable damage to myself, resulting in heavy bouts of depression and anxiety. For years, I relied on antidepressant and antianxiety medications to keep me in a somewhat balanced state, but after cultivating a dedicated meditation practice I eventually found myself at a place where, under doctor supervision, I was able to taper off the medication and no longer needed it.

Let me make it perfectly clear, however, that there is absolutely *nothing* wrong with taking prescribed medication for conditions like anxiety, depression, and so forth. I recognize that they were very necessary in my life at that time, as I was very chemically off-balance. There is nothing *unspiritual* about taking prescribed medication when needed, because our own mental and emotional well-being *must* come first before we can truly help others.

Whether we are on medication or not, meditation practices will certainly help us to not only cultivate more calm in our lives, but also to handle things like stress, anxiety, and depression in gentler ways. For the benefit of those who are new to meditation, I'm providing these simple guided instructions for the practice of vipassana.

A Guided Vipassana Meditation

There's no shortage of "spiritual positions" suggested for meditative practices, but really, as long as you keep your spine straight, without being overly tense or rigid in your posture, you'll be fine. You can sit with your legs crossed in half or full lotus position, sit upright in a chair with your feet on the ground, or lie down flat on your back (before lying down, however, be mindful of whether or not you're tired, as it can be easy to fall asleep during meditation).

As far as mudra (hand) positions go, put them wherever feels right to you. You can place them in your lap, palms up, one on top of the other; you can place them palms down on your knees; or fuck it, you can even make those silly circle things with your fingers, which has become the quintessential consumer vision of what we're supposed to look like while meditating. It really doesn't matter, though. Whatever feels most comfortable for you is the right position. Once you've got the hands figured out, close your eyes.

Next, bring your awareness to your Buddha belly (or chiseled vegan abs), roughly two inches above your navel, along the vertical midline of your body. Remember that this is not an exact science, so just bring your awareness to somewhere in that area, wherever feels right for you. (Note: Bringing attention to the tip of your nose, just inside your nostrils, as you breathe in and out, is also an anchoring point in vipassana. If that feels more natural to you, go with it!)

As you bring your awareness to your belly, you'll begin to notice that, as you breathe in, your abdomen expands, and as you breathe out it contracts. The movements of expanding and contracting are often referred to as "rising" and "falling," and are used as anchoring points to focus on during practice.

As your abdomen expands, observe its motion from beginning to end. Then do the same as it contracts. It's that simple. Your breath, and the rising and falling of your abdomen, happen naturally, with no conscious effort on your part, so as you bring your awareness to the rising and falling motions, they anchor you in the present moment. If you find you're having difficulty perceiving the rising and falling movements, it may help to place your hand on your stomach to feel them more clearly.

It also helps to recognize that the rising and falling are actually separate movements. There is a moment, after the abdomen has expanded to its fullest, and just before it begins to contract, that it is completely still. Being vigilant in your awareness of this break point in the motion can be extremely helpful in keeping your concentration focused, as it keeps your awareness centered.

As you practice vipassana meditation, thoughts are bound to arise. When this happens, it's important not to mentally beat yourself up. Simply acknowledge the thoughts whenever you catch yourself drifting, and let them go as you bring your awareness back to your abdomen. Our aim in this practice is to cultivate awareness, not to think, so do your best to just be.

As we continue with our practice, we want to experience the knowing of our abdomen rising and falling. This knowing is experienced as nonverbal, pure awareness. The same goes for anything else that may come up during practice. Regardless of what it is, we know it with pure awareness in the moment, and then we let it go.

While vipassana definitely isn't overcomplicated by any means, it's also probably not as easy as you think. There's a reason vipassana is not only practiced by those new to meditation, but longtime meditators as well: it's a tried and true way to anchor our attention here and now in the present moment, which helps us to let go of unnecessary nagging worries, fears, frustrations, and so forth.

When we come to vipassana as a beginner, it can be of serious benefit to mentally label the rising and falling movements of our abdomen as they occur. These mental notes support mindfulness by increasing momentary concentration. So for the duration of the abdomen's expansion, we can mentally say "rising," and for the duration of the abdomen's contraction, we can mentally say "falling." The tricky part here is that, while we're mentally repeating the words "rising" and "falling" over and over, we want to keep our awareness on the sensation of the abdomen rising and falling and not the mental repetition of the words. Remember, our aim is to *know* the experience itself.

Once we feel confident in our awareness of anchoring into the rising and falling sensations without mentally labeling them, we can then let go of that part of the practice. Remember, this is not a race, so if you find you're months (or even years) into the practice and mental repetition of the words "rising" and "falling" still helps, then stick with it. There's no face to be saved here, and anyone who brags about their meditation practice obviously still has plenty of work to do.

As you continue with vipassana, here are a few more things to be aware of:

- Make sure the breath flows naturally. Do not try to control it.
- Be aware of your abdomen moving, but do not visualize it. The experience should be similar to that of a buoy floating naturally up and down in the water. Shit, now you're going to visualize a buoy during practice, aren't you? Well, do your best not to and try to let it all be as natural as possible.
- While vipassana is most conducive in a quiet setting during formal practice periods, it can be done anytime and anywhere. Whether you're sitting at your desk at work, riding on a bus, at the movies, or wherever, anytime you bring your awareness to

the natural movement of your abdomen rising and falling, you're mindful in the moment and thus you're practicing vipassana.

- Vipassana, or any form of meditation for that matter, will naturally cultivate a greater sense of calm, peace, and mindfulness in your everyday life. However, it will take some time, so have patience and be gentle with yourself.

Some people, including myself, have reacted to meditation in the exact opposite way they thought they would. Typically, we expect a sense of peace and calm. Instead of floating in the clouds with Buddha, we may find ourselves mentally clawing our way out of a Freddy Krueger nightmare. For some, painful thoughts and memories may arise, sparking an emotional response that can make for an unpleasant experience. While this is not the case for everyone, it does sometimes happen, so if you find yourself having one of those experiences, *do not* let it scare you away!

The uncomfortable times in meditation offer us the opportunity to do some truly wonderful work. As we sit and allow uncomfortable thoughts and emotions to play themselves out, with the understanding that they *cannot* harm us, we're allowing healing to unfold naturally. We're allowing the pain and hurt from days, weeks, months, and even years ago to be released in whatever way our body, and meditative experience, sees fit.

allow uncomfortable thoughts and emotions to play themselves out

At the conclusion of meditation practice, it is sometimes suggested (though not required) to make an aspiration based on any merit we cultivated during our time spent in quietude, as an offering of peace, love, and harmony to all beings. Here is an example of something simple you can recite (though you can use any words that resonate with you).

May all beings be free from danger.
May all beings be free from mental suffering.
May all beings be free from physical suffering.
And may all beings know peace.
Om

Through the practice of vipassana, we begin to stop associating so strongly with the mental constructs of who we think we are, which allows us to stop taking ourselves so goddamn seriously. We learn to embrace our imperfections exactly as they are and as a part of who we are. We can celebrate the fact that we're imperfectly perfect, and together we can make a big mess of our imperfections. So let's get messy. Let's rekindle the carefree inner child that many of us have been suppressing for far too

rekindle the carefree inner child

long now, because that too is part of being an indie spiritualist—embracing our most authentic selves in a fearless yet lighthearted and carefree way.

2

MAHASATI MEDITATION

A particularly dear meditation practice that I enjoy sharing with others is called *mahasati* meditation. It comes from the Buddhist tradition, but you do not need to be Buddhist to reap its amazing benefits. I say this meditation is particularly dear to me because I learned it **while I was in detox** while I was in detox, from a clinician assistant who just so happened to be Buddhist, and has subsequently become a dear friend. He learned it from a Laos monk who lived in caves for thirteen years and now resides in Connecticut. I've since had the privilege of practicing this meditation with the monk himself on numerous occasions, which only adds to its specialness for me.

Mahasati is a term originating from Pali (which is an ancient Indian language). *Maha* means "great" or "big," while *sati* means "self-awareness" or "mindfulness." Together, mahasati means "great, total, or perfect self-awareness." When we work on cultivating this self-awareness, we become more mindful of our physical actions, and the more we practice, the more our mindful state will become second nature.

While I'm going to share with you the formal hand movements of mahasati, the practice is actually done anytime we're aware of what we're doing, or present in the moment. The intentional practice of these hand movements, however, facilitates that awareness in our daily lives. Here are a few things to be aware of before starting:

allow the movements to be natural

When practicing, keep your eyes open and fixated on something that won't distract your attention (for example, the floor approximately three feet in front of you usually works well). While moving your hands and arms, be aware of the movements. There's no particularly formal way to position your body; you can sit however feels right for you—on the floor, in a chair. or you can even practice this while standing or lying down.

Whichever body position you choose, do your best to allow the movements to be natural. Do one at a time, being aware of each as you're doing it. Be comfortable and relaxed, and try not to go into this practice with the desire for any expected results. The joy is in the doing and being, and in time it will naturally benefit your everyday life.

Movement 1: Rest your hands palm down on your thighs.

Movement 2: Turn your right hand onto its side, with the awareness of what you're doing. Make the movement mindfully and slowly, and then stop. Do not mentally tell yourself to turn your hand, but rather be aware of the movement as it happens.

Movement 3: Mindfully raise your right hand up, and then stop.

Movement 4: Lower your right hand down to your abdomen allowing it to rest, and then stop.

Movement 5: Turn your left hand onto its side, and then stop.

Movement 6: Raise your left hand up, and then stop.

Movement 7: Lower your left hand down on top of your right hand, which is resting on your abdomen, and then stop.

Movement 8: Move your right hand up to your chest, and then stop.

Movement 9: Move your right hand out, and then stop.

Movement 10: Lower your right hand onto its side on the thigh, and then stop.

Movement 11: Turn your right palm down, and then stop.

Movement 12: Move your left hand up to your chest, and then stop.

Movement 13: Move your left hand out, and then stop.

Movement 14: Lower your left hand onto its side on your thigh, and then stop.

Movement 15: Face your left palm down, and then stop.

Repeat movements one through fifteen as long as desired, maintaining a continuous flow of rhythmic movements.

Watch me demonstrate, rather comically at first, this mahasati meditation (which took me at least twenty takes). http://www.youtube.com/watch?v=lJsCe9MwFok.

3

KARMA YOGA & THE THIRTY-TWO
Body Part Meditation

Ａll of the practices provided in this book are offered as agents
of change, but the following two practices I've found particularly useful in dealing with the darker aspects of life discussed in this
book. The first practice, karma yoga (selfless service) is an action
practice, while the second practice is a meditation on impermanence
and our thirty-two body parts (sometimes referred to as "meditation
on repulsiveness").

Karma Yoga

In the traditional sense, karma yoga is helping others as an offering
to God. It's selfless service, which means that, while we're performing
the action, we do our best to come from a place of connectivity with
all others who are involved. It's great for people to perform random
acts of kindness, but at the same time it's also very easy to get lost
in the ego satisfaction of thinking of ourselves as someone special
for doing something kind for another. It's not that those acts are not
special, because anytime someone performs an act of kindness for

someone else, *it is*. However, in karma yoga, identifying with a sense of how "special" we are rather than selflessly doing the act creates a disconnect between our self and the other person, which hinders our opportunity to experience the Divine connection of Oneness with all those involved.

One of the easiest ways to begin practicing karma yoga is through volunteer work. Volunteer opportunities are readily available at places like hospitals, hospices, nursing homes, local nonprofits, mentoring programs, and many more. If you're not familiar with opportunities in your area, check out your favorite Internet search engine and you'll have no problem finding some! If volunteering isn't your thing, you can also do things such as paying the toll for the car behind you, changing a tire for someone in need, or helping someone reach an item in a grocery store. Even a simple act like picking something up for someone who's dropped it can certainly be karma yoga when done from the heart.

If you make yourself available for service, life will gladly present you with opportunities to act. And as you help others for no other reason than from the kindness of your heart, you'll find yourself anchored into the warmth of your heart center on a much more frequent basis!

The Thirty-Two Body Part Meditation on Repulsiveness

The Buddha taught monks a technique for contemplating their thirty-two body parts, in an effort to release attachment to their physical bodies by recognizing their impermanent nature in a very deep and personal way. In the thirty-two body part meditation, we contemplate the body and each of its parts, as well as the repulsive nature they can have, in an attempt to reverse the intrinsic, material love and identification we've placed on them. It's not that loving our bodies is wrong, but when we're completely identified with them, it distorts our perception of our true Self, significantly handicapping our experience of reality.

The practice is very simple. We contemplate our body's thirty-two parts and their impermanent nature, distancing ourselves from them. We begin at the top of our head, systematically moving down to our feet and then back to the top again. If you'd like to really get into the repulsive pirouette in thinking, you can incorporate the contemplation of your skin being full of pollutants.

The thirty-two body parts are as follows:

- Hair of the head, hair of the body, nails, teeth, skin
- Flesh, sinews, bone, marrow, kidneys
- Heart, liver, membranes, spleen, lungs
- Bowels, intestines, gorge, dung, brain
- Bile, phlegm, pus, blood, sweat, fat
- Tears, grease, snot, spittle, oil of the joints, urine

What I've come to learn about this meditation is that it's not really about being repulsed by our bodies, because, if that were the case, we'd merely be replacing attachment with aversion. Rather, the goal is to come to experience our bodies as something neutral. And with that experience and understanding, it becomes easier to not take so seriously these material selves we've been conditioned to believe we are.

I've also found this practice to significantly help with self-esteem issues. Through the application of this meditation, and the recognition of the very frail and fleeting nature of the human body, it becomes much easier to understand that we really are imperfectly perfect, exactly as we are in this very moment, regardless of whether we think we're too tall, short, fat, skinny, or any other such nonsense.

4

SELF-ENQUIRY (ATMA VICHARA)

As we begin to experience love as our core essence, rather than whatever it is our egoic thoughts have been telling us we are (our name, job, body type, and so forth), it's an opportunity to establish a deeper connection with our authentic and Divine essence. Trying to elaborate on this essence in words can be a very tricky thing to do, because, well, how does one speak about the unspeakable? It's like when you ask someone to explain the Tao, the most common answer you're likely to hear from students is, "The Tao that can be spoken of is not the eternal Tao." For example, *Hardcore Zen* author Brad Warner had a similar dilemma while trying to explain his first insight experience to me:

> There was a moment when a lot of factors about my zazen practice came together all at once. I had one of those so-called "transformative moments" or whatever the learned people are calling them this week. I haven't been able to look at life the same way since. There's no way to communicate what that experience was. I have met a handful of people

in my life who've had similar things happen to them. And sometimes I can speak with those people about it. I find it's utterly impossible to say anything meaningful about it to anyone who hasn't gone through it themselves. Even the language I'm forced to use to discuss it is really misleading. It can't even be called an "experience." I can't say I've "been through it." All of that makes no sense. But there are no other linguistic formations available.[18]

Brad did a pretty damn good job of putting it into words, and, from my own experience, I'd definitely agree; it's rather difficult to put into words the whole God/Being/Divine/Oneness thing. So with that being said, I'd like to share with you a practice that I've found to be very helpful in experiencing this unspeakable for ourselves, because, as with basically everything else I've talked about in this book, the importance always lies within the experience rather than the conjecture and semantics that some students spend inordinate amounts of time bickering about.

This is a process called *Self-enquiry*, which I learned about through reading much of Sri Ramana Maharshi's literature. Regarding this practice and its transcendental nature, Sri Ramana said:

This ghostly ego which is devoid of form comes into existence by grasping a form; grasping a form it endures; feeding upon forms which it grasps it waxes more, leaving one form it grasps another form, but when sought for it takes to flight.

Only if that first person, the ego, in the form "I am the body," exists will the second and third persons (you, he, they, etc.) exist. If by one's scrutinizing the truth of the first person the first person is destroyed, the second and third persons will cease to exist and one's own nature, which will then shine as one, will truly be the state of Self.

The thought "I am this body of flesh and blood" is the one thread on which are strung the various other thoughts.

Therefore, if we turn inwards enquiring "Where is this 'I?'
all thoughts (including the "I"-thought) will come to an end
and Self-knowledge will then spontaneously shine forth."[19]

So the practice is based on asking oneself the question "Who
am I?" At first glance, this may sound like a very elementary question, with a simple answer. For example, I could say: "I am Chris
Grosso. I have tattoos and am still **"who am I?"**
an exceptionally nice guy. I laugh at
inappropriate humor, listen to Black Sabbath, yet still have a dedicated
meditation practice and work diligently on cultivating loving-
kindness for myself and others." On the surface, these things
describe some of who I am, but what they don't address is the deeper
context of who I *truly* am underneath that. These descriptions fail
to acknowledge the real *me* that existed before this physical manifestation that is Chris Grosso, and which will continue to exist after the
physical manifestation ceases to be.

Before we get into the practice itself, let's quickly break down the
gross (physical) body, as part of this Self-enquiry process is to systematically negate the things we typically use to identify ourselves.

We have five cognitive senses: hearing, touch, sight, taste, and
smell. We have organs of speech, locomotion, grasping, excretion,
and procreation. We also have a mind that thinks and brings awareness to this experience of our physical manifestation. When all of
these things are removed from the equation, however, all that is left
is pure awareness, and that is our true Self. So with that being said,
here's an abridged version of the Self-enquiry technique.

- Our individual (or ego) self is nothing more than a thought or
  idea. This is the "I"-thought, which originates in our core, what
  Buddhism calls the heart center, located on the right side of the
  chest, though many spiritual traditions also consider this area of
  the body to be our spiritual center.
- From our core, the "I"-thought rises to our brain, making itself
  at home while declaring, "I am this body."

- Thus is created the illusion of mind and an individual self that inhabits our bodies, and under its own direction, appoints itself controller of our thoughts and actions.
- The "I"-thought does this by identifying itself with every thought and perception as it arises in our awareness. This creates a habit of associating *everything* with this "I"-thought; for example, "*I* can't wait to see Slick Rick, Naughty by Nature, EPMD, and Big Daddy Kane's Old School Hip Hop tour next week." Or, "*I* can't believe *I'm* still annoyed at how bad Star Wars Episodes I, II, and III were (okay, I actually really like Episode III, whatever)."
- The way we begin to reverse this process is by depriving the "I"-thought of all that it identifies itself with. It's imperative to recognize the "I"-thought as being unreal in the first place, and that it can only *seem* to exist when it identifies with thoughts as they arise.
- So as we begin to disassociate from the "I"-thought and the thoughts it identifies itself with, a space is then created that allows for the "I"-thought to subside.
- We do this by bringing our awareness to the sensation of "I am" as it resonates within ourselves.
- As we root ourselves in the awareness of this internal sensation of "I am," we ask ourselves, "Who am I?" and "Where does this 'I' come from?" If we conduct this query in a fearless way, it's inevitable that we'll begin to recognize the "I"-thought's false nature, and it will then begin its return to our heart center.
- As we keep our awareness on the internal sensation of "I am," our Self guides the "I"-thought back to its place of origin, in our heart center.
- It's at this point that Self-realization ("I am that I am") occurs, and we lay aside the conditioned false idea that we are strictly an isolated, individual self.

To be brutally honest, this is a practice that is hard won and easily lost, but the benefits of applying it in our daily lives is beyond the worth of its application. As we begin to spend less time identifying ourselves as strictly physical beings, life becomes a much friendlier and more inviting experience. Things aren't always happening *to us* anymore; rather, they're just happening and we're along for the ride, watching it all go down. Sure, life will still hurt. There will still be painful events and undeniable tragedies that will shake us to our core. But underneath

Sure, life will still hurt

them, there will be a spaciousness that makes it all less personal. It is in this place that life, and everything it throws at us, becomes much easier and peaceful to work with.

5

LOVING-KINDNESS MEDITATION

Some of us have deep levels of self-loathing that have taken us to places that are even darker than just day-to-day mental shit-talking. We may have been abused growing up, picked on in school, sexually assaulted, or have abused drugs or alcohol. Whatever the reason, it can be that much more difficult for us to find a semblance of love and acceptance for ourselves, as compared with the average person. It's during these times, the times when I find my heart sinking for either myself or others who have gone through this kind of pain, that I'm reminded of a quote by Hafiz of Shiraz, in which he says, "I wish I could show you, when you are lonely or in darkness, the astonishing light of your own being."

Today I feel so grateful that I can honestly say I recognize many of my own good qualities. That's a huge step for a person like me, who's had serious self-love and respect issues throughout his life. I used to not have a single mirror in my apartment, because I couldn't stand the sight of myself. But today, more often than not, I'm able to look at the person reflecting back at me with love and compassion. This was not an easy task, nor did it happen overnight, but putting forth the effort to change my perspective was completely worth it. And a big part of the reason this change has taken place is thanks to the practice of loving-kindness meditation.

The reason I was able to connect with the loving-kindness meditation practice on such a deep level in the beginning was because it wasn't just about loving myself, but loving all beings. It taught me to balance the love of self and others, something I'd never previously been able to do. In the beginning, I'd definitely say my loving aspirations were 98 percent toward others and only 2 percent toward myself, but as I continued with the practice those percentages began to even themselves out. Today, I still sometimes find the scales tipping in favor of others. When I do, I use that as an opportunity to remind myself that we really are all One, which means that, by not showing myself the same love I would show you, well, I'm limiting love for us all, and that's not cool.

From Noah Levine to Pema Chödrön and many more, loving-kindness has become a very popular practice to teach. After spending years with it myself, I completely understand why. The following is how I've come to use it in my life, but it's not a rigid set of instructions. The general structure from beginning to end should be followed, but if you'd like to change certain words so that you're able to connect with them more deeply, by all means, go right ahead.

Loving-Kindness Meditation

Begin by closing your eyes and taking two or three long, slow, deep breaths into your belly. We do this simply to relax ourselves and bring our awareness into the here and now. The loving-kindness aspiration always begins with yourself, which can be tricky for those like myself who have self-love issues. We've come this far, though, so please stay with me and just do your best. As you work with this practice, you'll cultivate a deeper sense of joy, compassion, equanimity, and friendliness toward yourself (and others).

After you've developed some semblance of loving-kindness toward yourself, move on to someone you love. This person can be a spouse, child, spiritual teacher, and so forth. Anyone you can love easily is suitable. With eyes closed, envision this person and send them loving-kindness from your heart to theirs. We also mentally say something to the person as well, such as, "May you enjoy true love and happiness in your life." But again, whatever words you feel most comfortable using are just as suitable.

Next, we move on to sending loving-kindness to a friend or relative—a person we feel goodwill toward. Continue to hold an image of them in your mind and mentally send them a loving aspiration.

We then think of someone we're neutral toward. This can be the person who serves us coffee at the local coffee shop, our mailman, or anyone we're typically impartial toward. Picture them in your mind and send them a loving aspiration.

From the neutral person, we then move on to a difficult person. For example, this can be a boss, coworker, in-law, or anyone who is a source of irritation in our lives. Hold the image of them in your mind and, no matter how difficult it may be, do your best to send them a sincere loving and kind aspiration.

(Some teachers leave the loving-kindness practice at just making those aspirations, which is perfectly fine. You will certainly begin to experience changes in your life from working with only those. Other teachers incorporate two more steps, which I personally use and find beneficial, so here they are.)

After we've sent loving-kindness to ourselves, a loved one, a neutral person, and a difficult person, we then hold all of these people in our hearts and minds simultaneously, and say, "May I, my loved one, neutral person, and difficult person all enjoy happiness and the root of happiness." (Make sure to use their actual names and not those generic descriptive terms.)

Our final step is to picture our love engulfing all of these people, and then spreading to include the entire earth and the farthest reaches of space, as we send loving aspirations to all beings in all places and times.

As with any transformational practice, deep, lasting change takes some time to accomplish; however, you will likely begin to experience results from the loving-kindness meditation after your first practice. You may feel lighter or have a general sense of well-being. Or, you may possibly feel nothing at all in the beginning. At the very least, you can rest assured that, since you've taken time out of your day to make positive aspirations for yourself, others, and the universe as a whole, the love you cultivated and sent out *will* come back to you in one way or another, probably sooner than later.

When we establish a more loving relationship with ourselves, one in which we're able to let the mental chatter play out however it's going to, while knowing better than to take it seriously, our lives *will* become more inspiring and beautiful. There are so many goddamn brilliant things happening all around us every day, so many miracles happening right in front of us, but we're usually too busy mentally shitting on ourselves (or others) to notice them.

Some of my hardcore/punk cred is going right out the window by saying all this fruit-loopy, happy stuff, but whatever; it's a sincere truth that I've come to experience firsthand. And I feel it's really important for me to let you know that it's not only *possible* for you to experience this yourself, but it's also *much* easier than you probably think. When you begin to work with this practice, and with whatever other practices in this book resonate with you, you really will begin to find yourself experiencing authentic love more of the time, as well as smiling playfully at the ridiculous things your mind says to you. And another bonus is that the negative chatter many of us experience will become less frequent, replaced with more compassionate thoughts and loving aspirations for ourselves and others.

Life's a pretty amazing thing, and its magnificence is happening around us all the time in the simplest of ways. It's up to us, however, to decide: Are we going to continue on autopilot, allowing our

own our shit and take the power back

incessant negative thoughts and emotions to dictate our mental and emotional well-being? Or are we going to own our shit and take the power back? We've already wasted enough time feeding into thoughts of lack, doubt, insecurity, and unworthiness, so I implore you to ask yourself, when is enough going to be enough?

Practices

The following is a mixed bag of both traditional and nontraditional practices I've personally found to be beneficial on my path, which have allowed me to remain completely true to myself, while still honoring others on their paths—spiritual or otherwise. Some of them may resonate with you, some may not, and some may leave you wondering whether I'm dead fucking serious in offering them as suggested "spiritual practices." I'll just go ahead and answer that right now by saying yes. Yes, I'm dead fucking serious about them (in a completely lighthearted and unserious way, of course).

I've said it before, but I feel it can't be repeated enough: I truly believe that anything we do with even a hint of mindfulness, and from the place of a sincere and loving heart, is spiritual, even writing a spiritual book while listening to Mobb Deep . . . like I am right now.

6

GOING TO A CONCERT

Hell, yes, as crazy as it may sound to some, we can find spirituality at things such as concerts—rock, classical, jazz, hip-hop, or otherwise. As I've already shared, one of my most spiritual experiences happened at a Van Halen concert, of all places. When we experience music in a live setting, any live setting—from a small jazz club to a punk/hardcore show in a basement or VFW hall, all the way to seeing iconic legends at Red Rocks or Madison Square Garden— once the music starts, it connects all those in attendance in a very universal way. As the music plays, we unite in our Collective Consciousness, regardless of political, spiritual, or other types of belief, which, only moments prior to the beginning of the show or concert, may have caused separation between us and others in attendance. Music is definitely a universal language, and when we experience it live it encourages us to let go of everything and just be there in the moment, in the spirit of celebration with others.

7

VISITING A MUSEUM OR GALLERY

Making the trip to a museum or art gallery is not only for dating or school field trips anymore! The ancient art, sculptures, and so forth are a surefire way to connect to a deeper state of being within ourselves. The unspeakable beauty of these artifacts and imagery can definitely take us to a place of mindfulness and awe, which in turn reunites us with the amazing events of their history.

8

MALA OR ROSARY BEAD WORK

Mala (or rosary) work is simply the repetition of prayers, mantras, or aspirations, recited while moving the beads of a necklace or bracelet through our thumb and middle finger in the direction of our self, one by one, until we reach the large "Guru" bead in which we stop, turn the mala around, and start over. As each bead passes through our fingers, we mentally or verbally recite the words of our mantra or prayer, allowing our attention to naturally fixate itself on nothing but the words and whatever experience they subsequently bring us to.

Here are a few of the more common prayers and mantras traditionally used:

Om Mani Padme Hum

The meaning of *Om Mani Padme Hum* is difficult to translate into a phrase or sentence, but it's typically associated with compassion, as it is believed to invoke the attention and blessing of Chenrezig, who is the embodiment of the compassion of all the Buddhas.

His Holiness the Dalai Lama explains the Om Mani Padme Hum mantra as follows:

> It is very good to recite the mantra Om mani padme hum, but while you are doing it, you should be thinking on its meaning, for the meaning of the six syllables is great and vast ... The first, Om symbolizes the practitioner's impure body, speech, and mind; it also symbolizes the pure exalted body, speech, and mind of a Buddha. The path is indicated by the next four syllables. Mani, meaning jewel, symbolizes the factors of method: [the] altruistic intention to become enlightened, compassion, and love. The two syllables, padme, meaning lotus, symbolize wisdom. Purity must be achieved by an indivisible unity of method and wisdom, symbolized by the final syllable hum, which indicates indivisibility. Thus the six syllables, om mani padme hum, mean that in dependence on the practice of a path which is an indivisible union of method and wisdom, you can transform your impure body, speech, and mind into the pure exalted body, speech, and mind of a Buddha.[20]

Gate Gate Pāragate Pārasamgate Bodhi Svāhā

This mantra originates from *prajñāpāramitā* (perfection of wisdom) sutras in Buddhism, and translates to: "Gone, gone, gone beyond, gone utterly beyond, Enlightenment hail!"

we are one with the eternal everything

Practice of this mantra is believed to guide those who use it past ego identification to a deep place of calm, bringing our awareness to the place where we are one with the eternal everything. I've personally had wonderful results from continued use of this mantra and find myself returning to it frequently in both good times and bad.

Hail Mary/Our Father

These two prayers/mantras are among the most well-known, and while some of those reading this book may have an aversion to Catholicism (trust me, I totally get it), I've found there to be a very healing and humbling quality to the following words when the dogma attached to them is laid aside.

Hail Mary, full of grace. The Lord is with thee. Blessed art thou amongst women, and blessed is the fruit of thy womb, Jesus. Holy Mary, Mother of God, pray for us sinners, now and at the hour of our death. Amen.

Our Father, Who art in heaven, hallowed be Thy Name; Thy kingdom come, Thy will be done, on earth as it is in heaven. Give us this day our daily bread, and forgive us our trespasses, as we forgive those who trespass against us; and lead us not into temptation, but deliver us from evil. Amen.

If formal isn't your thing, it's perfectly acceptable to repeat words such as "love," "peace," "thank you," or whatever else resonates with you. The main purpose of mantra and prayer is to cultivate mindfulness and a greater sense of peace and serenity in our daily lives, which *will* be accomplished regardless of the semantics of the words we use.

9

JOURNALING

Journaling is one of the most therapeutic gifts we can offer ourselves, especially for those of us who have trouble confiding in others. As we lay pen to paper, we can write anything, in complete confidence, while also allowing it to be an act of purging. Once the words have been written, we can offer them to whatever Higher Power we believe in, or we can rip the pages from our journal and burn them. We can even simply do nothing, and let them be, knowing we've gotten them out. If you prefer to write just for the sake of writing, that is also an amazingly spiritual experience, as it lets your insides out in a completely unfiltered way. And whether it's your conscious intention or not, you'll often be facilitating self-healing in the process.

10

PRAYER

Similar to meditation, there are numerous ways to pray, with none of them being any more correct than the other. The important thing to remember is that there really is no right or wrong way to pray. The purpose of prayer is to establish a conscious connection with something greater than ourselves and, keeping in line with the running theme of all the aforementioned practices, as long as we approach prayer with a sincere heart and intention, there's no way we can go wrong. A form of prayer I've had wonderful results with, which I find very reminiscent of vipassana meditation, is called contemplative prayer (also known as centering prayer). I was honored to receive a firsthand explanation and instruction regarding contemplative/centering prayer from the wonderful Trappist monk Father Thomas Keating in an interview I did with him some years ago. The following excerpt is from that interview:

> Centering Prayer is a contemporary term for an ancient and well-traveled Christian path toward contemplation. It is a practical way of cultivating interior silence based largely

on The Cloud of Unknowing for practical inspiration. It is suggested in a number of places in the Gospel, and especially in the classical invitation of Jesus when he said, "When you pray, go to your inner room, close the door and pray to the Father in secret, and the Father who sees in secret, will reward you." So what distinguishes it from other forms of prayer such as vocal prayers, aspirations, or reading the scriptures in a meditative way? All these practices are stepping stones to the silence of our own inner mysterious self, which is deeper than the senses, deeper than thinking, deeper even than consciousness itself.

The focus of Centering Prayer is to sit still and let go of the external senses and the interior dialogue that goes on almost uninterruptedly in our minds. Letting go of images, desires, memories, reflections, emotions, commentaries, judgments; in other words, the whole interior razzmatazz that goes on as we talk to ourselves about what's happening, and taking stock of our emotional reactions to events within and without. Sitting regularly (like everyday) gradually overcomes the tendency of our minds for non-stop thinking.

It may be a help to have some gesture by which we can renew our intention when thoughts become tedious, bombarding, or persecuting. In this prayer we learn that we're not our thoughts. We have them, but we need not identify with them. Little by little, their intensity begins to diminish as we cultivate our inner room (the spiritual level of our being).

We recommend 20–30 minutes twice a day, because we're dealing with habits that have a physiological basis in the brain and which react to stimuli in a habitual way. Over time we are able to undermine habitual modes of thinking formed by our self-made self in early childhood, which tries to squeeze happiness from the gratification of our desires for the symbols in our culture of survival and security, power and control, and affection and esteem. Thus part of the process of Centering Prayer consists in accepting the coming to awareness of our attachments to these emotional needs and moderating them by our rational faculties that hopefully are developing in childhood, adolescence, and adulthood. The capacity for emotional sobriety belongs to everybody in the human family and leads to a fully human response to the adventure and goodness of the gift of human life.[21]

The capacity for emotional sobriety belongs to everybody

11

CREATING ART

The beautiful thing about art is that anyone can create it at any time using virtually anything. You don't have to be an artist in the traditional sense to use art as a means of connecting with spirit. Whether you're doodling spiritual imagery, or collaging pictures of things you're interested in—tattoos, flowers, skateboards, bands, nature, spiritual teachers, or eclectic random images—it's all relevant and it's all art. The same goes with painting. Even if you completely suck at it, like I do, it's still a lot of fun to break out some paint like you did when you were a kid and just go to town, not caring about the final result.

If painting is not your thing, how about going outside and creating visual art in nature, using whatever you find in front of you: rocks, sticks, leaves, and so forth. This may sound ridiculous and silly, but until you've actually given it a try, don't knock it. My amazingly **anything can become art** talented wife Jenn Grosso was instrumental in teaching me that anything can become art. She is the craftiest woman I know, who creates all sorts of weird and cool art pieces—from tiny shrines to collages and much more—often using the most random of things (check out her Flickr page for some very cool examples: http://www .flickr.com/photos/jenngrosso/).

Doing things out of our traditional norm is a great way of loosening up and not taking ourselves too seriously, which also helps us become more vulnerable in our spiritual practice.

12

VISIT A CHURCH, MOSQUE, MONASTERY, OR SACRED PLACE

This is one of the simplest ways to connect with traditional spirituality with very minimal effort, because you'll be engulfed in an intentionally spiritual setting. Making a mini pilgrimage to a local church, monastery, mosque, or temple is something you can do alone or with others, if for no other reason than to experience amazing artwork, statues, and spiritual and religious traditions in general, which can be moving even if only on an aesthetic level. I made it clear earlier that besides meeting some great people, I've also had some shit experiences in these settings too, but over time I've learned to not care if I catch someone giving me dirty looks or whatever. I'm there to connect with my deeper self, so I focus on that. They can spend their time however they'd like.

13

YOGA

Traditional asana (body positions) yoga has become wildly popular, especially here in the West over the last decade, so if you're interested, it shouldn't be difficult to find a class in your area. It's true, I rib yoga sometimes in my writing, but it's always in good fun. In all seriousness, I'm completely aware that the yogic practice of asana can be very beneficial. I mean, anything that guides practitioners to focus both their consciousness and body in ways they're not traditionally used to, taking the individual outside of the norm, has got to be good, right? And from what I've been told by some of my yoga-teacher friends, asana is doubly beneficial because it helps practitioners adapt to life's everyday challenges as they arise, rooting them more firmly in the practice of working with unfamiliar and challenging situations and territory.

taking the individual outside of the norm

It's also very important to note that, while asana yoga is very popular, it's only one form of yogic practice. Other forms of yoga include bhakti yoga (devotional yoga), jnana yoga (path of wisdom yoga), karma yoga (yoga of selfless service), and more.

Often, people combine various types of yoga, though it's not necessary. I'm personally preferential to bhakti yoga, because I thoroughly enjoy performing kirtan, as well as jnana, since I'm a full-on book nerd and love feeding my brain. Those are just my preferences, however, and hey, maybe you have no interest in any form of yoga whatsoever, and that's totally cool too.

full-on book nerd

14

TALKING TO PEOPLE

Each person has a story to tell. Although not everyone's story ends up in your history book, each person's story fits into the history of that time. Like a web, each person is affected by what happens—and, in turn, leaves his or her mark upon the world. One of the best ways to gain perspective about yourself is by asking questions of others who have seen some shit and know what they're talking about.

At least, that's what I've done. The Indie Spiritualist website has provided me the chance to interview a lot of people who've significantly impacted me throughout my life and continue to help me open my eyes to new ways of seeing the world. In preparation for this book, I also interviewed many people from all walks of life, to give me a little perspective on what it's all about, amassing a large, varied, intriguing, sad, happy mountain of wisdom, and I'm glad I did. From Indo-Tibetan Buddhist scholar Robert Thurman to *Night of the Living Dead* zombie legend George A. Romero (and many other diverse individuals in between), I've learned—through the art of interview—many intriguing little nuances about both myself and this thing we call life. Here's just a small sample of the questions I asked (feel free to steal for your own purposes):

To whom and/or what do you attribute the person you are today?

What are some of the musical albums, musicians, or bands that have impacted your life, and in what way?

What is one of the most shocking experiences you've ever had?

What is one of the most beautiful experiences you've ever had?

What is one of the most defining moments in your life, and why?

What do you believe are the benefits, if any, versus the dangers of mind-altering drugs?

What are some films you'll never forget seeing for the first time, and why?

Does God exist? If so, in what capacity? If not, why not?

What do you think is your greatest contribution to humanity?

What does the human experience mean to you?

Then sit back and listen. You'll be amazed by what you learn.**

** Visit this link http://theindiespiritualist.com/category/10-questions-series/ to read some of the interviews I mentioned above on TheIndieSpiritualist.com, including Bernie Siegel, Fred Alan Wolf, don Jose Ruiz, and more.

15

GRATITUDE

I'd certainly be remiss if I didn't take a moment to talk about gratitude before this book comes to a close. For many, gratitude doesn't come easily. This is understandable, because life can be really fucking difficult and leave us in extremely stressed-out places, places where it's hard to recognize the gift in even the simplest of luxuries we have every single day.

By this point in the book, you obviously know I've been through some shit in my life, but it's that "shit" that makes gratitude such an easy practice for me today. I suppose, when you've lived a lifestyle where throwing up on oneself in bed isn't completely out of the norm, it makes it easy to be grateful for the so-called little things in life. But no one needs to hit such a low as that in order to make gratitude an integral part of their daily lives.

So as far as the practice itself, it's quite simple, really. All we do is make our best effort to be as grateful, for as many things as we can, throughout as much of our day—start to finish—as possible. For example, if you catch yourself enjoying the smell of fresh-cut grass, mentally say "thank you" for enjoying that lovely smell, and feel gratitude. Reading poems from Bukowski? Be grateful that such a brilliant writer lived and that his work found its way into your

be grateful for goddamn Dave Grohl

life, again, by mentally acknowledging it and saying "thank you." New Foo Fighters record coming out? Awesome! Be grateful for goddamn Dave Grohl for being such an inspiring dude as well as a part of both Nirvana (haters gonna hate) and Foo Fighters. "Thank you."

On an even simpler day-to-day level, do you have soap you wash your hands with, a toilet to shit in, shoes for your feet, a refrigerator for your food? Things like these get taken for granted on a daily basis by most people. We forget there are so many others—the world over—who don't have what we could consider "minor" conveniences.

My last endorsement for this gratitude thing is that it also cultivates mindfulness. I went through a period where, for a few months, I kept a little note in my pocket that read, "Right now, look around. What are you grateful for?" And every time I'd dig in my pocket, looking for something, and my fingers touched the note, I'd stop, look around for a moment, and mentally say "thank you" for whatever I felt grateful for in my immediate surroundings. And trust me, there's *always* something to be grateful for.

The experience of gratitude I was cultivating eventually began seeping more and more into my daily life, to where I no longer needed that note, because it had become second nature to me.

I know a lot of the shit I've written about in this book is gritty, because, well, that's been a big part of my experience these thirty-five years. And while, yes, the pain of the past still visits from time to time, I'm not going to pretend like things aren't beautiful more often than not these days, because that couldn't be farther from the truth. "Thank you."

Eclectic Multimedia
Suggestions

As I mentioned in the introduction, a big part of the spiritual camaraderie I experienced early on in my search was based on a common interest I shared with others when it came to bands, movies, books and so forth, much of which had little to do specifically with "traditional spirituality."

These various arts offer us a unique opportunity to come together with people who we otherwise may have never gotten to know. I can't tell you how many times I've become friends with someone after finding out we had a shared interest in some of the same obscure (and sometimes not so obscure) bands, movies, and books.

Obviously there's plenty of other ways to meet and bond with people, but I've shared so many amazing experiences with individuals equally as passionate about the arts as I am, that I thought it worthy of addressing before this book comes to a close.

And so it's in that spirit that I offer you some of my personal favorites—the books, movies, and albums that have deeply touched my life and subsequently become the catalysts for many of the amazing shared experiences I've had with others.

16

BOOKS

Reading is an invaluable part of our spiritual practice. While yes, the books and words we read are simply signposts guiding us inwards, guiding us home, they are still wonderful catalysts in taking us deeper into our practice and experience. Traditional spiritual material is not the only form of spiritual reading, either. Authors such as Charles Bukowski, Neil Gaiman, Hunter S. Thompson, H. P. Lovecraft, William S. Burroughs, and many others, while typically not considered spiritual at all, have personally helped me process some of my own unsavory experiences in life, through their gut-wrenchingly honest writing styles. As I've said repeatedly throughout this book, the ability to look at things from nontraditional spiritual angles can help give us insights we might have otherwise overlooked if we'd stayed within the confines of what's typically considered "spiritual." Here are a few suggestions of both traditional and non-traditional pieces of literature which have greatly influenced my own path. (Note: I can't begin to tell you how difficult it was to narrow this down to only a few titles, as I own literally hundreds of books. That being said, regarding spiritual books, I opted to leave off the classics such as the Bhagavad Gita, the Dhammapada, *Tao Te Ching*, *A Course in Miracles*, *The Gnostic Gospels*, and so forth, as I feel like they kind of go without saying (but with that being said, I still highly recommend reading all of those!).

Cutting Through Spiritual Materialism, **Chögyam Trungpa Rinpoche**. This book is the quintessential punk-rock thesis on spirituality. It cuts through all of the bullshit of spiritual materialism by very clearly laying out the most common pitfalls that spiritual aspirants, both new and old, fall prey to time and again. I sincerely wish that every person interested in spirituality would read this book. It'd certainly help in laying aside so much of the dogmatic nonsense that causes separation between individuals.

Hell's Angels, **Hunter S. Thompson**. This author was a true independent spirit. In *Hell's Angels*, Hunter S. Thompson takes readers into a world that the majority of us will never experience—one filled with drugs, sex, alcohol, crime, and the lifestyle of an outlaw biker gang. I appreciate this read, as it's a real eye-opener into a way of life that, while quite normal for those who live it, would typically scare the shit out of those who don't. The only thing I remotely miss in *Hell's Angels* is the minor lack of "gonzo"-style journalism that Hunter Thompson later became so famous for in *Fear and Loathing in Las Vegas* and *Fear and Loathing: On the Campaign Trail '72*. Regardless, this is still an absolutely exceptional read.

The Spiritual Teaching of Ramana Maharshi, **Ramana Maharshi**. *The Spiritual Teaching of Ramana Maharshi* is a book of transcribed conversations between Ramana and spiritual seekers from around the world. Ramana teaches from a place that transcends religious differences, thus making this book an amazingly accessible read for all seekers and easily one of the most important books I've read (and read, and read, and read).

Burning Fight: The Nineties Hardcore Revolution in Ethics, Politics, Spirit, and Sound, **Brian Peterson**. For those looking for a more definitive history of the punk/hardcore movement, you'd probably want to try *American Hardcore: A Tribal History* by Steven Blush. For those such as myself who came up in the '90s hardcore music scene, however, this book is it. For me, this book personifies the underground, independent music culture that, as I've already talked about throughout this book, heavily impacted my sense of self and individuality. Featuring a ton of commentary from those who were there, including interviews with some of the most important '90s hardcore bands—Inside Out, Threadbare, 108, Deadguy, Coalesce, Unbroken, Rorschach, Burn, Groundwork, and many others—this book is an amazing nostalgic reflection of one of the most important times in both my life and the lives of others who were there.

Be Here Now, **Ram Dass**. Whenever Ram Dass's classic book *Be Here Now* comes up in conversation, I usually can't help but laugh, as I'm reminded of the fact that I've bought this book well over a dozen times, yet don't own a physical copy myself. It's one of those books I'm always so excited to give people to read, because I know how life-changing it was for me, and hope it will be the same for them. It's just that I never have the heart to ask for it back. In *Be Here Now,* Ram Dass offers readers a spiritual cookbook filled with various practices; psychedelic art, accompanied by brilliantly insightful writing within the artistic theme; and an amazing mini memoir, in which he shares his transformation from Harvard professor (then known as Richard Alpert) to spiritual renunciate in India. Ram Dass shares almost unbelievable stories about traveling to India and meeting his guru, Maharaj-ji (Neem Karoli Baba). Many of the stories are funny, touching, mesmerizing, and completely paradigm-shattering. There's so much more to this book, including an amazing 108 pages in the middle, which are filled with crazy artwork and mini stories, lessons, mantras, and more.

The Last Night of the Earth Poems, **Charles Bukowski**. The brilliance in this book, as well as in every other thing Bukowski wrote, is his authenticity, rawness, and gifted understanding of the craft. Bukowski is just about the only writer who can make me laugh out loud one minute and have my skin crawling in disgust the next. All of Bukowski's work is really quite fucking brilliant, and though Bukowski wouldn't give a shit about the following statement, he's as punk rock as it gets.

A Brief History of Everything, **Ken Wilber**. I mean, the title says it all, doesn't it? From pre-cradle to post-grave, Ken Wilber—in *A Brief History of Everything*—gives us an entertaining and mostly accessible account (it can be academic at times, but it's definitely worth sticking with) of men, women, and all sentient beings in existence in the universe. Wilber also touches on topics that include multiculturalism, ecology, gender wars, and environmental ethics, and he does an amazing job of connecting the dots between not only all religious and spiritual traditions, but also between the arts, music, business, and so much more. I absolutely love this book—along with the rest of Ken's bibliography. I feel forever indebted to Ken for opening my eyes to the true depths of life, love, and integral well-being.

Revolutionary Suicide, **Huey P. Newton**. *Revolutionary Suicide* is part manifesto, part philosophy, part history, and *full* revolution. Huey P. Newton was one of the original founding members and leaders of the controversial late-1960s organization, the Black Panther Party. This book shines a very raw light on the racial heinousness of the '60s and '70s, yet is still just as relevant today as it was when it was first written, because revolution is never not an important topic!

The Places That Scare You, **Pema Chödrön**. Pema Chödrön's no-bullshit approach to spirituality is obviously influenced greatly by her teacher Chögyam Trungpa Rinpoche, which makes her doubly awesome in my book. In *The Places That Scare You*, Chödrön teaches that we already have the wisdom, inherently within us, to face life's difficulties, but that we usually block it with patterns rooted in fear. This book has helped me immensely in accepting life as it is, both the good and bad times, while doing my best to find the beauty in it all.

***H. P. Lovecraft: The Complete Fiction*, H. P. Lovecraft.** I was like a kid in a candy store when Barnes and Noble released this complete work from the brilliant horror/science-fiction writer H. P. Lovecraft. Written during the 1920s and '30s, some of the language and style may be unappealing to some readers, but I personally find it adds to the brilliance of the experience, which is that of something completely unfamiliar to our normal lives—a creepy, haunting, and chaotic experience of the mind.

***Living Buddha, Living Christ*, Thich Nhat Hanh.** Thich Nhat Hanh is one of those people I just want to scoop up and give the biggest hug ever to. And now that we've cleared that up, in *Living Buddha, Living Christ*, Thich Nhat Hanh does an amazing job of sharing the similarities between Buddhist and Christian practices, comparing the Holy Spirit with Buddha Nature, and much more. The message of this book is both timely and timeless, and is an amazing treatise on interfaith acceptance, respect, and celebration! Hanh also wrote a follow up book titled *Going Home: Jesus and Buddha as Brothers*, which is another exceptional read.

***Junky*, William S. Burroughs.** In one of Burroughs's most celebrated novels, *Junky*, he tells the fictionalized story of himself, a white male who, after an introduction to drugs (or "junk," as he calls it), finds himself in a vicious cycle of addiction. This isn't an easy read, but an amazing eye-opener for sure, and one that's eloquently written in Burroughs's infamous style. And for what it's worth, Burroughs was raging against the machine while Zack de la Rocha was still in diapers (definitely no disrespect to Zack, though).

The Book, **Alan Watts**. In *The Book*, Alan Watts emphasizes the importance of a personal experience, an experience he describes as "knowing who or what you really are behind the mask of your apparently separate, independent, and isolated ego." Watts draws quite a bit on the Vedanta tradition of non-dualism, which obviously is something that resonates very deeply with me. And while this book definitely isn't a light read, I believe it can have a profound impact on a reader's life, especially upon reading it for the second, third, fourth time, and so on.

The Big Book of Alcoholics Anonymous, **Dr. Bob Smith and Bill Wilson**, and *Narcotics Anonymous Basic Text*. Though I read both of these books because I live with the disease of addiction, I recall my mother saying she believes that anyone who reads them— addict/alcoholic or not—could benefit greatly from what they say, and I couldn't agree more. While yes, both books are certainly tailored to those who struggle with alcoholism and addiction, there is applicable insight and wisdom for anyone who's ever struggled with, well, let's just say "anything." And I think most of us fall into that category.

Honorable Mentions

Breaking the Habit of Being Yourself, Dr. Joe Dispenza
House of Leaves, Mark Z. Danielewski
Finding Freedom, Jarvis Jay Masters
American Gods, Neil Gaiman
Dharma Punx, Noah Levine
Tipping Sacred Cows, Betsy Chasse
Last Call for the Living, Peter Farris
The Tibetan Book of Living and Dying, Sogyal Rinpoche
The Skateboard: The Good, the Rad, and the Gnarly: An Illustrated History, Ben Marcus
I Am That, Sri Nisargadatta Maharaj
Live from Death Row, Mumia Abu-Jamal
The Disappearance of the Universe, Gary Renard

A Gradual Awakening, Stephen Levine

Fuck You Heroes, Glen E. Friedman

The Sermon on the Mount According to Vedanta, Swami
 Prabhavananda

Fight Club, Chuck Palahniuk

The Doors of Perception, Aldous Huxley

Slaughterhouse-Five, Kurt Vonnegut

Walden, Henry David Thoreau

Cash: The Autobiography, Johnny Cash

The Awakening of Intelligence, J. Krishnamurti

A Feast of Snakes, Harry Crews

All Are Called and *Few Choose to Listen*, Kenneth Wapnick

There Is No God and He Is Always with You, Brad Warner

Integral Life Practice, Ken Wilber, Terry Patten, Adam Leonard, and
 Marco Morelli

Radical Acceptance, Tara Brach

Death by Black Hole, Neil deGrasse Tyson

The Wise Heart, Jack Kornfield

17

FILM

From documentary to horror, comedy to drama, there's something for everyone in the world of film. As with books, I find inspiration and insight from very diverse styles, so here's another eclectic mix of some films for your viewing consideration.

Say Anything. Lloyd Dobler is looking for a "dare to be great situation," and I mean, at our core, aren't we all? This movie always inspired me, because while on the surface, sure, it's about the slightly below average guy who goes after and gets the untouchable girl. But on a deeper level, it's every great story ever told—overcoming insurmountable odds, achieving the impossible, and following your heart *until the very end* . . . all in the name of love . . . love and kickboxing, *the sport of the future.*

The Matrix. If you haven't seen *The Matrix* by now, chances are that you probably never will. However, allow me to advocate on its behalf for a moment. It incorporates elements of Buddhism, Vedanta, and a slew of other spiritual undertones, as the hero, Neo

(Keanu Reeves), becomes awakened from the dream reality that he believed in his entire life, thanks to mentor Morpheus (Laurence Fishburne). So with that as the story's underlying premise, plus insane action, great special effects, and insightful metaphysical dialogue throughout the entire film.

What the Bleep Do We Know!? Now in its tenth anniversary of bridging the gap between science and religion, *What the Bleep!?* remains a vital voice in the celebration of unity between two of life's greatest influences. Sure, it may have taken some liberties in its implications, as the film's co-creator Betsy Chasse has acknowledged in recent years, but the message that everything isn't always as it seems stays completely intact. Watch this film and be prepared to see life through an entirely new set of eyes.

Donnie Darko. Bringing together time travel, apocalyptic visions, one-liners like "suck a fuck," and a borderline-schizophrenic leading character named Donnie (played by Jake Gyllenhaal), who also just so happens to hallucinate and see a life-size rabbit/reptilian creature named Frank—*Donnie Darko* is a cult movie enthusiast's wildest dream. If that brief description did nothing to pique your interest, definitely do not bother watching it. For everyone else, go watch this movie now!

Kumare. *Kumare* is the true story of a false prophet and an amazingly important exploration into just how easy it is to take advantage of those on spiritual paths. I talked earlier in the book, in the vignette titled "Holy Grail Sale," about the vulture-esque nature of some companies who have their hand in spirituality, and *Kumare* is exactly in line with that message. This is an important film for all spiritual aspirants to see, *especially* those new on the path.

Zeitgeist: The Movie. This film is important on many different levels. It starts out by completely pulling the rug on early religion, and how it became a big business based on fear campaigns. It then goes on to tackle and present startling information regarding the 9/11 tragedy, the federal reserve, government officials in general (nothing new there, however), and other scary signs of the time. There are also two subsequent films, *Zeitgeist: Addendum* and *Zeitgeist: Moving Forward*, which are also both worth checking out as well.

The Big Lebowski. Jeff Bridges's character Jeffrey "The Dude" Lebowski was such a laid back, inadvertent Zen teacher in this film that it sparked the recent release of a book titled *The Dude and the Zen Master*, written by The Dude himself, Jeff Bridges, along with Zen master Bernie Glassman, and has received critical acclaim across the board. As for the film itself, well, it's something you have to see to understand, man.

Abide as the Self: The Essential Teachings of Ramana Maharshi. This is a wonderful documentary, narrated by Ram Dass, about the life and teachings of the brilliant Vedanta teacher Sri Ramana Maharshi. You can watch it for free on Youtube by searching the keywords "Abide as the Self." Watching this documentary will be an hour of your life entirely well spent.

Halloween (1978 version). This is still my all-time favorite horror movie. *Halloween*, which stars Jamie Lee Curtis in her acting debut, is the quintessential indie horror movie, and it's worth checking out for more than just a good scare. I find the film's villain, Michael Myers, to reflect both the calm in this world through his Zen-like nature while stalking his victims, as well as the world's insanity through his stab-happy murder tendencies. Plus, Dr. Loomis (Michael's psychiatrist in the film) is equal parts awesome as he is bat shit crazy.

Religulous. Love him or hate him, Bill Maher has always been one to raise some important questions, and in *Religulous*, he goes straight for the jugular. Facing off against Christians, Jews, Muslims, and more, Maher addresses religious fanaticism and the ways in which it's contributing to the world's problems rather than solutions. Maher, taking a page from Jesus himself, leaves no stone unturned in this documentary.

Star Wars (Episodes IV–VI). When it comes to *Star Wars*, there usually isn't any middle ground; you either love it or hate it. As for me, well, I absolutely love them (the original three, anyway). Similar to *The Matrix*, *Star Wars* has it all—heavy spiritual elements, sci-fi action, light sabers, kick-ass bounty hunters, snarky robots, blaster pistols, epic space battle scenes, and Darth Motherfucking Vader!

Honorable Mentions
Beats, Rhymes & Life: The Travels of A Tribe Called Quest
Ram Dass: Fierce Grace
The Royal Tenenbaums
Evil Dead I and *II*
Rising Son: The Legend of Skateboarder Christian Hosoi
Where the Buffalo Roam
Kids
Peaceful Warrior
The Quantum Activist
The Shawshank Redemption
Thrive
The Breakfast Club
Waking Life
Natural Born Killers
Eternal Sunshine of the Spotless Mind
Dawn of the Dead (1978 version)
The Boondock Saints
Anchorman
Taxi Driver
What Dreams May Come
Barfly

18

MUSIC

Okay, as if it wasn't tough enough to narrow down some books and films for you, I'm going to try and name some of my top albums!? A borderline impossible task, but I shall do my best. Similar to what I did with the book section, I'm leaving off the "should go without saying" bands and musicians like Johnny Cash, Black Sabbath, John Coltrane, Nick Drake, Led Zeppelin, Al Green, Townes Van Zandt, Pink Floyd, Bob Dylan, and countless others. I should mention, however, that I give a somewhat lengthy "thank you" to the musicians, bands, and artists who've inspired me throughout my life, in the acknowledgements section at the end of this book, so for further recommendations, please look there (and thanks to my copyeditor Sheila Ashdown for dealing with that ridiculousness).

Ágætis Byrjun, **Sigur Rós.** *Sigur Rós* creates the kind of ethereal music I'd expect to be playing while visiting other astral planes, entering the gates of heaven, or upon awakening to an enlightened state, particularly on this, their second album, *Ágætis Byrjun*.

The Cold Vein, **Cannibal Ox**. What happens when you put together the brilliant minds of Vast Aire, Vordul Mega, and El-P? You get my pick for best hip-hop album ever. Yes, I know that's a controversial statement to hip-hop fans, but hey, it's just my pick and I'm not saying I'm necessarily right (though I'm pretty sure I am). Combining raw, discordant, sci-fi laced beats with esoteric, relevant, and insightful lyrics, this is real hip-hop . . . important hip-hop, and a soundtrack for ingenuity and individuality.

Northern Failures, **Cable**. Cable is a band dear to my heart, not only because they're from my own home state of Connecticut, but also because they've made amazing music for over a decade now. They've been pioneers in the post-hardcore music scene since the mid '90s and have never been afraid to try something new with their sound, basically saying fuck all to music's often-limited status quo. *Northern Failures* was a pivotal shift in their style from chaotic and screamy to full-on rock—dark, gritty, and very heavy rock. Bonus points for the fact that they're all seriously good dudes too.

Pilgrim Heart, **Krishna Das**. *Pilgrim Heart* is the Krishna Das album I referenced earlier in my piece titled "The Entanglement Theory of Kirtan, Punk Rock & Hip-Hop," and has become a staple in my "go-to for spiritual uplifting" music file. On *Pilgrim Heart* (along with all of KD's other releases), he sings with a passion and sincerity that musically mirrors the very same passion and sincerity of his guru Maharaj-ji's love.

Vaudeville Villain, **Viktor Vaughn (aka MF Doom)**. MF Doom is an acquired taste for many hip-hop fans, and his alter ego, Viktor Vaughn, is definitely no exception. The *Vaudeville Villain* album, however, is one of the most original and inspiring pieces of hip-hop music I've ever heard. Very little of it makes sense in traditional hip-hop language—many of the time signatures and beats are all over the place, as are Doom's lyrics. However, it all comes together in an inspiringly original way that I appreciate for its sincere creativity.

Slip, **Quicksand**. This album was a game changer in the hardcore music scene, to say the least. The lyrics were introspective in a time when social and political musings were the typical punk/hardcore norm; the music maintained a very hard yet emotional edge while being neither hardcore nor emo; and the band even went on to find some minor commercial success. I had the privilege of seeing Quicksand on the very first Vans Warped Tour in 1995. And while I've unfortunately never seen them in a smaller club setting, their set at the Warped Tour is still one of the greatest live performances I've seen to date.

Through Silver in Blood, **Neurosis**. *Through Silver in Blood* provided me with probably my earliest transcendental experiences. I remember making a forty-five-minute commute to and from college in New Haven back in 1996–97; oftentimes I'd put this album on and, before I knew it, I would be arriving at my destination. It definitely wasn't that I was lost in thought, like most people find themselves while driving, but rather, I'd completely lose myself in the heavy, hypnotic, and pulsing rhythms of their songs, which often surpass the ten-minute mark. Awesome.

Midnight Marauders, **A Tribe Called Quest**. All of Tribe's albums are hip-hop classics. However, *Midnight Marauders* is the Tribe record I find myself coming back to most often. Incorporating a heavy jazz influence, along with the soulful vocal styling of emcee Q-Tip, the unapologetic vocal approach of emcee Phife Dawg, and beats from DJ/producer Ali Shaheed Muhammad, *Midnight Marauders* is a near-perfect hip-hop album.

Jawbox, **Jawbox**. Jawbox guitarist J. Robbins has always been somewhat of a guitar hero to me. His driving and intense guitar style has always spoken to me in a very deep way, for whatever reason. On their self-titled album, Jawbox gives listeners nine brilliant songs, songs that break the barriers of what indie rock or post-hardcore guitarists are supposed to write and play, with not a single one of them a throwaway.

***Fixation on a Coworker*, Deadguy.** I own a Deadguy T-shirt that says "death to false metal," and that's exactly what these guys were all about. Brutally raw, heavy, and honest, both musically and lyrically. To this day, I'm still waiting for a hardcore album as good as *Fixation on a Coworker* to come out.

***Do You Know Who You Are?*, Texas Is the Reason.** For a band that only put out one full-length album, Texas Is the Reason's impact on the emo music scene is legend. *Do You Know Who You Are?* is filled with catchy, emotionally driven songs that are just as applicable for someone dealing with the pain of a breakup as they are for someone driving down the highway with their windows open on a perfect summer afternoon. Bonus points for the fact that this album has amazing production, courtesy of J. Robbins (Jawbox).

Honorable Mentions
Illmatic, Nas
Feeling Older Faster, Threadbare
Isn't Anything, My Bloody Valentine
Badmotorfinger, Soundgarden
Deltron 3030, Deltron 3030
How to Clean Everything, Propagandhi
You Are Freaking Me Out, Samiam
Autumn of the Seraphs, Pinback
Fear of a Black Planet, Public Enemy
1000 Hurts, Shellac
Spanaway, Seaweed
The Mosquito Control, Isis
The Family Sign, Atmosphere
It's a Wonderful Life, Sparklehorse

Until Your Heart Stops, Cave In
Either/Or, Elliott Smith
Entheogen, Bloodlet
93 'Til Infinity, Souls of Mischief
Yank Crime, Drive Like Jehu
Five, Empty Flowers

Seriously, I could be here all day, so I'll just stop right now.

PARTING WORDS

So there you have it, a mini smorgasbord of spiritual musings and suggested traditional and nontraditional spiritual practices to get you started. I really can't reiterate enough that anything that brings you to a place of deep inner-connectedness, as well as helps to cultivate mindfulness, peace, and joy in your life, *is* a spiritual practice, no matter how unconventional it may seem.

But that's just my two cents. How about you? What have you found that has and hasn't worked for you, both spiritually and otherwise? What are some of your favorite books, movies, and albums? What spiritual practices work for you? I invite you to join me at TheIndieSpiritualist.com, facebook.com/XchrisGrossoX, and twitter.com/XchrisGrossoX so we can get deeper into this conversation. Because while, sure, this book **no matter how unconventional** obviously had to incorporate personal things about me, I truly believe that, as a whole, this really has very little to do with me. Rather, it's a familial thing, it's about *us*—our pain and struggle, our hope and redemption.

I really didn't want to end this on a cliché note, but fuck it; it really is like Gandhi said: We *can* be the change we wish to see in the world. Each voice and life can make a difference, but when those voices and lives are united in the celebration of love and acceptance, well, you know what happens when you throw more wood into the fire! Christians, atheists, Buddhists, Jews, Muslims, Hindus, Wiccans, agnostics, punk rockers, hip-hoppers, skateboarders, yogis, athletes, business men and women, rich, poor, and whoever else—why not come together and live our lives in such a way that the examples of love and acceptance we set are impossible for others to ignore?

This. Shit. Is. Doable.

May it start here by my saying, I truly love you all. From the bottom of my heart to yours, thank you. I'm honored to have spent this time with you, and humbly invite you to join me in keeping this thing moving onward and inward.

ACKNOWLEDGMENTS

Before I can thank anyone in particular, I have to give thanks to the twelve-step fellowships for being a huge catalyst in helping me live a healthy and productive life and making all of this possible, one day at a time. And with that being said, I've got a lot of thanks to give, so here we go . . .

It is with heartfelt gratitude that I offer thanks to my literary agent and dear friend, Michele Martin. Your guidance, support, love, and insights have helped me find, time and again, the inspiration to believe in this vision and see it to fruition. Thank you so much. And to Steve Harris, thank you so much for all of your help in this endeavor as well.

To Marci Shimoff and Kim Forcina, thank you both so much. Your guidance, support, and love has meant so much and inspired me in countless ways. Thank you.

My sincerest thanks to Emily Han, Henry Covey, Cynthia Black, Lindsay Brown, Jackie Hooper, and the rest of my family at Beyond Words, Atria Books, and Simon and Schuster for believing in this vision, and your tireless efforts in helping to make it a reality. It's been a true blessing to create this book with you.

Big thanks and love to my family: Brenda and Lawrence Grosso, Peter and Francine Lui, Jay, Catie, and Addison (Danger Dog) Grosso, Allison Lui and Will Campbell, Lynde Dodge, Carrie, CJ, Ethan, Ella, and Eva Pendleton, Eddie, Justin, and Shiloh Dodge, and Scott, Lynn, and Scott Dodge Jr.

Thanks for all the love and support: Justin Mehl, Alanna Kaivalya, Jessica Durivage-Kerridge, Lisa Marie Selow, Justin Good, Jen Taylor, Amy Scher, Dan O'Brien, Ken Wilber, Tommy Rosen, Lissa Rankin, Stephen and Ondrea Levine, Jarvis Jay Masters, Noah Levine, Betsy Chasse, MC Yogi, Kayla de Both, Breeze Floyd, Andrew Cvercko, Kelley Hagemes, Kate Bartolotta, Jenn Cusano, Heather Church, Jodi Geoghan, Bernie Romanowski, Cheryl Guertin, Harriet Cianci, Ri Stewart, Carl Kerridge, Gary and Cindy Renard, Aaron Turner, Sara DiVello, Kaye McCarthy, Sera Bishop, Jay Barnes, Mike Banfield, Jennifer Colon, Ilene Mitnick, Alli Baldwin, Robin Fox, all of my amazing Dharma Punx/Against The Stream friends (too many to name, but you know exactly who you are!), Laurie Gelston-Alt, David Muckle, Steve Karp, David Nielsen, Peter Farris, Andy Nelson, Darrell Tauro, Ryan Keefe, Craig Gilbert and Gretchen Werda, Daryl Anderson, Jon Laneri, Jeannette Duckson, Jodi Smith, Joe Reed, Martine Persico, Nelda Street, Wendy & Michelle Thiebeault, Kathy, Ken & Mickey Durivage, Jessica Elizabeth Donofrio, Sean Crook, Patrick Bisaillon, Brian Bisaillon, April Anderson, Sophie Tong, Ron Tannebaum, Ken Pomerance, Jessica Pimental, Andréa Balt, Tanya Lee Markul, Sharon Pingitore, Vic Szalaj, Randy Larsen, and all of the amazing friends I've made through my social media networks, thank you so much for the love and support. And a very special thank you to *you* for taking the time out of your busy life to read these pages.

Thank you to The Sanctuary at Shepardfields for serendipitously finding your way into my life at precisely the right time. Thank you to Yoganonymous, *Where Is My Guru*, Rebelle Society, The Good Men Project, Suicide Girls, Huffington Post, Intent Blog, and Elephant Journal for allowing me to share myself with others through your media. Thank you to The Path Less Traveled Records for giving my band, Womb of the Desert Sun, the time of day. Thank you to Phoenix Ink Tattoo, Precise Piercing and Tattoo, and Kustum Kulture Tattoo (RIP) for all of the ink and laughs throughout the years. Thank you to Powell-Peralta for being Powell-Peralta, my favorite skateboarding company since 1986! Thanks intherooms.com for all the support you provide recovering addicts with. A big thank you to the Northern Middlesex YMCA (particularly Melanie Carfora, Amy Cardoza, Sue Rumanoff, Ceara Ladue, Chaelyn Lombardo, Kevin Cassesse, Patrick Connelly, Tony Sharillo, and Michele Rulnik).

And of course, a very sincere thanks to the bands, musicians, and emcees who've inspired me throughout my life, in ways that are beyond words. The following is an *extremely* abridged list: 108, A Tribe Called Quest, Al Green, Ashes, At the Drive-In, Atmosphere, Barkmarket, Bear vs. Shark, Big L, Black Flag, Black Sabbath, Black Sheep, Bloodlet, Blueprint, Bluetip, Bob Mould, Born Against, Brother Ali, Burn, Buzzov*en, Cable, Cage, Candiria, Cannibal Ox, Cap'n Jazz, Cave In, Cavity, CCR, Coalesce, Company Flow, Converge, Cursive, CunninLynguists, Daughters, De La Soul, Deadguy, Deftones, Deltron 3030, Dessa, The Dillinger Escape Plan, Dinosaur Jr., Dissolve, Don Caballero, Doomtree, Dr. Dre, Drive Like Jehu, Drowningman, Earth, Eazy E, Empty Flowers, EPMD, Engine Kid, Erik B. & Rakim, Explosions in the Sky, Faith No More, Falling Forward, Felt, Floor, Foo Fighters, Fu Manchu, Fugazi, Gangstarr, Glassjaw, Grade, Groundwork, Handsome, Hannah's Field, Harvey Milk, Helmet, High on Fire, His Hero Is Gone, Hot Water Music, House of Low Culture, Hum, Iceburn, Immortal Technique, Indian, Inside Out, Iron & Wine, Iron Maiden, Isis, Jai Uttal, Jawbox, Jeru the Damaja, Jesu, The Jesus Lizard, JFA, Jimmy Eat World, John Coltrane, John Frusciante, Johnny Cash, June of '44, Kaki King, Keelhaul, Kiss It Goodbye, Kool G Rap, Kool Keith, Krishna Das, KRS-One, Lifetime, Low, Marvin Gaye, Mastodon, Mamiffer, MC Yogi, Melvins, Metallica, MF Doom, Miles Davis, Minor Threat, Mobb Deep, Mogwai, Mr. Bungle, Múm, My Bloody Valentine, Nas, Naughty by Nature, Neurosis, Nick Drake, Nirvana,

Old Man Gloom, Om, Outspoken, Overcast, Pantera, Pete Rock & C. L. Smooth, The Pharcyde, Pinback, POS, Propagandhi, Public Enemy, Quicksand, Refused, Retribution Gospel Choir, Rorschach, Samiam, Sage Francis, Seaweed, Sebadoh, Shellac, Shudder to Think, Sigur Rós, Slayer, Slick Rick, Souls of Mischief, Snapcase, Soul Position, Soundgarden, Sparklehorse, Split Lip (Chamberlain), Statue, Suicidal Tendencies, Sunny Day Real Estate, Swans, Tad, Team Sleep, Texas Is the Reason, Threadbare, Today Is the Day, Torche, Townes Van Zandt, Unbroken, Undertow, Unsane, Wrench in the Works, Zao.

INDIE SPIRITUALIST
Playlist Index

Womb of the Desert Sun

"Invocation" by Womb of the Desert Sun, from *Invocation: Our Dying Days*.

"Transistor" by Womb of the Desert Sun, from *Where Moths Eat and Worms Destroy*.

Ambient Solos

"All About Us"
"Places That Scare You"
"The Complete Fiction"
"The Last Night of the Earth"
"Hand of the Host"

Acoustic Solos

"A Little Less Like Dying"
"Cardboard Suitcase"
"Drawing Static"
"Perils of the Living"

"Rising/Falling"
"Scream Phoenix"

Videos
Alanna Kaivalya and I playing at Kripalu.
Mahasati meditation.
Treach from Naughty by Nature shout-out. Hip Hop Hooray . . . Ho!

Interviews
Noah Levine interview on *Where Is My Guru* radio show.
Ram Dass interview for the *Where Is My Guru* radio show.
Jarvis Jay Masters interview for TheIndieSpiritualist.com.

NOTES

1. Jarvis Jay Masters, interview, The Indie Spiritualist website, January 29, 2013, http://theindiespiritualist.com/2013/01/29/finding-freedom-an-interview-with-author-buddhist-and-san-quentin-death-row-inmate-jarvis-jay-masters/.

2. Nate Newton, interview, The Indie Spiritualist website, May 8, 2012, http://theindiespiritualist.com/2012/05/08/mackaye/.

3. Ian MacKaye, interview, ibid.

4. Ruby Warrington, "The New Mantra: Replacing 'Om' with 'Glam,'" The New York Times (January 9, 2013): http://www.nytimes.com/2013/01/10/fashion/the-new-mantra-replacing-om-with-glam.html?smid=fb-share&_r=1&.

5. Mike Vallely, interview, The Indie Spiritualist website, February 4, 2012, http://theindiespiritualist.com/2012/02/04/vallely/.

6. Aaron Turner, interview, The Indie Spiritualist website, November 6, 2010, http://theindiespiritualist.com/2010/11/06/aaron-turner-of-isis-speaks-with-the-indie-spiritualist/.

7. Ibid.

8. Chögyam Trungpa, *Cutting through Spiritual Materialism* (Boston, MA: Shambala Publications, Inc., 2002), 13.

9. Pema Chödrön, "The Heart Sutra: A Teaching of the Sutra of the Heart of Transcendent Knowledge," Shambala.org, 2006, http://www.shambhala.org/teachers/pema/heart_sutra1t.php.

10. Lama Surya Das, "Who and What Is Buddha, Really?" *Huffington Post* (April 4, 2010), http://www.surya.org/who-and-what-is-buddha-really/.

11. Jai Uttal, interview, The Indie Spiritualist website, October 9, 2012, http://theindiespiritualist.com/2012/10/09/jai-uttal/.

12. Sri Nisargadatta Maharaj, *The Experience of Nothingness: Sri Nisargadatta Maharaj's Talks on Realizing the Infinite* (Berkley, CA: North Atlantic Books 1996, 2007), 6.

13. "For me, I feel that my earliest use . . ." Jai Uttal, interview for book (2013).

14. Sogyal Rinpoche, *The Tibetan Book of Living and Dying* (New York, NY: HarperSanFrancisco, 1994).

15. Lissa Rankin, interview for book (2013).

16. MC Yogi, interview, The Indie Spiritualist website, July 20, 2012, http://theindiespiritualist.com/2012/07/20/yogi/.

17. Ibid.

18. Brad Warner, interview for book (2013).

19. Sri Ramana Maharshi, "Self-Enquiry: Theory," from David Godman, Be As You Are: The Teachings of Sri Ramana Maharshi, http://bhagavan-ramana.org/selfenquirytheory.html.

20. His Holiness the Dalai Lama, lecture given at the Kalmuck Mongolian Buddhist Center, New Jersey, transcribed by Ngawang Tashi (Tsawa) and Drepung Loseling, Mungod, India, http://www.sacred-texts.com/bud/tib/omph.htm.

21. Father Thomas Keating, interview, The Indie Spiritualist website, December 22, 2010, http://theindiespiritualist.com/2010/12/22/keating/.

ABOUT THE AUTHOR

Chris Grosso is the Spiritual Director of the interfaith center The Sanctuary at Shepardfields, a 501(c)(3) nonprofit land preserve that offers educational resources for personal transformation, community evolution, and environmental restoration. Chris also runs The Indie Spiritualist website, which interviews an eclectic mix of people from the worlds of **film, literature, music, skateboarding, art, spirituality** and more. In his spare time, Chris tours the country playing as part of a two-piece kirtan band with yoga instructor and New World Library author Alanna Kaivalya. Chris also makes up half of the two-piece doom band, Womb of the Desert Sun, on The Path Less Traveled Records. You can also catch Chris with segments on the *Where Is My Guru* radio show, as a monthly columnist with *Mantra Yoga + Health* magazine, writing for websites such as Huffington Post, Rebelle Society,

The Good Men Project, Yoganonymous, Elephant Journal, Intent Blog, and more, as well as speaking, leading workshops, or performing music in a city near you.

Connect with Chris online at:
Website: TheIndieSpiritualist.com
Facebook: facebook.com/XchrisGrossoX
Twitter: twitter.com/XchrisGrossoX
YouTube: youtube.com/drawingstatic
Womb of the Desert Sun: facebook.com/wotds and thepathlesstrav-eledrecords.com
Kirtan with Alanna Kaivalya: facebook.com/akandcg

INDIE SPIRITUALIST PLAYLIST
(Audio Download)

http://www.beyondword.com
/indie-spiritualist-playlist/

Track 1: "Invocation" by Womb of the Desert Sun, from *Invocation: Our Dying Days* (5:17)

Track 2: "Places That Scare You" (3:32)*

Track 3: "The Complete Fiction" (3:04)*

Track 4: "Drawing Static" (5:26)*

Track 5: "All About Us" (4:07)*

Track 6: "Perils of the Living" (4:46)*

Track 7: "A Little Less Like Dying" (3:06)*

Track 8: "Scream Phoenix" (4:28)*

Track 9: "Hand of the Host" (4:00)*

Track 10: "Cardboard Suitcase" (3:23)*

Track 11: "The Last Night of the Earth" (5:19)*

Track 12: "Rising/Falling" (4:52)*

Track 13: "Transistor" by Womb of the Desert Sun, from *Where Moths Eat and Worms Destroy* (4:38)

* Music by Chris Grosso